CHRISTIAN
RESPONSE
—————— to ——————
MENTAL
ILLNESS

MUTUAL CARE
IN THE BODY OF CHRIST

Martin & Deidre Bobgan
AUTHORS OF *PSYCHOHERESY*

Scripture quotations are taken from the Authorized King James Version of the Bible, except as otherwise indicated.

Christian Response to Mental Illness:
Mutual Care in the Body of Christ

Let the words of my mouth,
and the meditation of my heart,
be acceptable in thy sight, O Lord,
my strength and my redeemer.

Psalm 19:14

Table of Contents

Preliminary Remarks

Use of Terms

We use the term *mental illness* according to its common usage, even though we argue that it is a confusing, catch-all misnomer. Therefore we do not put quotes around *mental illness*.

Our references to psychiatry and psychiatrists are in relation to the psychotherapy they practice, unless otherwise indicated.

We use the terms *counselor*, *counselee*, and *counseling* when what we say is related to the psychological or biblical counseling movement, because these are their preferred terms. Whenever we use the term *counseling* by itself in reference to biblical counseling, it refers to problem-centered biblical counseling, and when we use the designation "problem-centered counseling" by itself, it refers to both psychological and biblical counseling.

When we use the word *problem* we are referring to those problems normally talked about in psychological or biblical counseling. They are the mental-emotional-relational-behavioral problems for which people seek counseling help.

All references to *biblical counseling* refer to the psychologically formatted counseling adopted by those in the biblical counseling movement (see Chapter 9). We will not use quotes around the word *biblical* when used with the word *counseling*, but let it be understood that, as we demonstrate in our writing, **biblical counseling is not biblical, because it is sinfully problem-centered like psychological counseling**.

Psychotropic Medications

We want to make it clear that we do not recommend that individuals get on or off psychotropic medications. We generally do not write about psychotropic medications, but we do say that such medications are grossly over prescribed and greatly over used. Through the collaboration of psychiatrists and pharmaceutical companies, psychotropic drugs have been unnecessarily foisted upon millions of naïve individuals. Mental disorder labels are often recklessly and fecklessly applied by doctors to people who are undeserving of them. Moreover, based upon recommendations from friends and pharmaceutical advertising, consumers request such psychotropic medications from their doctors, and doctors who are on tight timelines too readily prescribe them. There are many skeletons in the psychiatric closet of the past and too many questionable practices of today, including sometimes clandestine relationships between psychiatry and the pharmaceutical industry. **Nevertheless, all decisions regarding whether to take or stop**

psychotropic medications should be done only under the supervision of a medical doctor.

Use of the Word *Sin*

We often use the word *sin* or a variation of it, such as *sinful*. There are many definitions for *sin*. However, the definition we use is "disobedience to the Word of God." We have written about and given examples for the sinful conversations that occur in both psychological and biblical counseling. We do not use the word *sin* lightly. Nevertheless, after seeing and/or hearing literal counseling conducted by both psychological and biblical counselors, we conclude that these conversations are often sinful.

1

The Rise and Use of the Medical Model of Mental Illness

The Christian response to mental illness is one of the great tragedies to ravage the church today. This tragedy began with the rise of the medical model of mental illness. The medical model used in the world of medicine has been hopelessly hijacked by those in the field of mental illness. The implications threaten the very foundations of psychiatry, as they depend on the medical model for diagnosing and treating mental disorders. These implications also threaten the foundations of psychotherapy and the biblical counseling movement as they follow the psychological counseling format. The very terms *mental illness*, *mental disorder*, and *mental disease* have become a blight to society, as they have been misunderstood, misapplied, misconstrued, and misused by many in both society and the church.

Introduction

The purpose in writing this book is to encourage believers to minister to all who seek biblical, spiritual care,

including individuals who are suffering from mental illness or who are suffering from other mental-emotional-
behavioral issues, known in Scripture as trials and tribulations, without throwing them into an either/or category
(biological or spiritual). Therefore, we scientifically discredit the prolific, promiscuous, and popular use of the
metaphor *mental illness* and later reveal that **one does
not always need to know the answer to the following
question**: Do those individuals who suffer from mental-
emotional-behavioral symptoms or who have been diagnosed with a mental illness without objective biological
markers have a true disease needing medical treatment, a
psychological problem calling for the worldly system of
psychotherapy, or a spiritual problem needing a biblical
solution?

To help those who would give mutual care in the
Body of Christ, we describe the origins of the medical
model of mental illness and its numerous ramifications.
However, we reveal that, **in most cases** of personal ministry, it is both not possible and not necessary to know for
sure whether or not such disorders or challenges are the
result of an objective biological illness.[1] In this perilous,
peculiar, and puzzling area of not truly knowing whether
or not a mental-emotional-behavioral issue is biological
or spiritual, one can nevertheless assume that **people are
responsible for their behavior and can benefit from
biblical ministry** (see Chapter 7).

We recommend that Christians who minister to others begin with the understanding that individuals, regardless of their mental-emotional-behavioral symptoms or
designations, can be ministered to, **as long as a rational
conversation can take place and that the content of**

the conversation is undergirded by love and biblically-based.

In our past writings we have revealed the sinful nature of both the psychological and the biblical counseling that follows the conversational format of psychological counseling. Over the years we have exposed counseling conversations of both psychological and biblical counselors that violate biblical admonitions.

As we have said many times: The best way to recognize the unbiblical nature of psychological and biblical counseling that explores personal relationships is to read or hear and evaluate available literal, live (**not simply playacted**) counseling by using biblical standards. There one can see and hear how the counseling problems are discussed and what sinful conversations are actually involved.

To Christians who support, promote, or practice either psychological or biblical counseling, we continue to offer the following challenge: "Provide one live, literal (not enacted) psychological or biblical counseling session that does not violate Scripture." To date no one has been able to provide one for us! This is proof positive that Christians should not be involved with psychological (psychotherapy) or biblical counseling as participants or practitioners!

In contrast to the expectation and practice of the usual counseling sessions with sinful conversations, we encourage what the church has provided through the years—mutual care (see Chapter 10), in which believers minister care for one another and encourage fellow believers to know the Lord, believe His Word, and learn to walk according to their new nature in Christ, rather than according to the old Adamic nature. Such ministry is for all believers to give and receive within the Body of Christ.

History of the Medical Model

As we describe the history of the medical model of deviant human thinking and behaving from its beginnings to its present, be aware that there is, in most cases, a lack of objective biological markers for almost all the diagnoses. Research psychiatrist Dr. E. Fuller Torrey describes the earlier predecessors of the medical model as similar to, but not as sophisticated as the contemporary idea that "for every distorted thought there is a distorted molecule."[3] All the medical models of mental illness from the beginning are theoretical ideas that are not directly supported by objective biological markers. The early predecessors of the medical model of irrational thinking and behaving were based upon speculation and conjecture. In other words, they were hypothetical ideas that lacked scientific proof.

Four Humors

The origins of the medical model date back at least to the Greek theories of humors and their derivative personalities. From ancient times through the Middle Ages, physicians and philosophers used their understanding of the four humors (bodily fluids), the four temperaments, and signs of the zodiac to treat diseases and understand individual differences among people. Torrey says that in the Greek theory of humors, "Irrational behavior of various kinds was attributed to an imbalance of the humors—depression, for instance, was due to excessive bile."[4] However, the "imbalance of the four humors" as an explanation for irrational behavior is a hypothetical idea that is not scientifically provable.

Middle Ages (Circa 500 AD to 1500 AD)

During the Middle Ages the medical model declined and religion was used to explain deviant thinking and behaving. It was conjectured that the mental-emotional-behavioral deviancy of mankind was attributable to demons or evil spirits. Many symptoms of irrational thinking and behavior were described during this period of time, but no objective biological markers were needed as the speculation was that the symptoms were due to the spiritual world.

Renaissance (Circa the 14th through the 17th Centuries)

During the Renaissance religious explanations for deviant thinking and behaving ebbed and medical treatment began for those individuals suffering from irrational behavior. The thinking and behaving symptoms were considered medical illnesses, though usually no objective biological markers were named.

18th Century

Franz Anton Mesmer (1733-1815) was another contributor to the medical model. Mesmer believed that he had discovered the great universal cure of both physical and emotional problems. In 1779 he announced, "There is only one illness and one healing."[5] Unlike the bodily humors, Mesmer presented a hypothetical idea that an invisible fluid was distributed throughout the body. He called the fluid "animal magnetism" and believed that it influenced illness or health in both the mental-emotional and the physical aspects of life. He considered this fluid to be an energy existing throughout nature. He taught that proper health and mental well-being came from the proper distribution and balance of the animal magnetism throughout the body. All of this was based upon Mesmer's say-so.

Mesmer's ideas may sound rather foolish from a scientific point of view. However, they were well received by many at the time. Furthermore, as they were modified, they formed much of the basis for present-day psychotherapy. The most important modification of mesmerism was getting rid of the magnets. Through a series of progressions, the animal magnetism theory moved from the place of the physical effect of magnets to the psychological effects of mind over matter. Thus the awkward passing of magnets across the body of a person sitting in a tub of water was eliminated and all that was needed to cure the irrational disturbance was a conversation.

Mesmer's far reaching influence gave an early impetus to scientific-sounding religious alternatives to Christianity. He also started the trend of medicalizing religion into treatment and therapy. Nevertheless, he only gave the world a false religion and a false hope. Distinguished Professor of Psychiatry Thomas Szasz describes Mesmer's influence this way:

> Insofar as psychotherapy as a modern "medical technique" can be said to have a discoverer, Mesmer was that person.... Mesmer stumbled onto the literalized use of the leading scientific metaphor of his age for explaining and exorcising all manner of human problems and passions, a rhetorical device that the founders of modern depth

psychology subsequently transformed into the pseudomedical entity known as psychotherapy.[6]

This was a pseudomedical entity because Mesmer still maintained his idea of "one illness, one healing" and the "animal magnetism" that flowed through the body, even when the magnets were no longer necessary for cure. Only the words between the counselor and client were needed. Mesmer created a mechanistic medical model built on symptoms, but absent objective biological markers, that produced the counseling movement that followed. The counseling that followed and continues right up to the present day deals with symptoms through a hypothetical framework for cure without the necessary objective biological markers to qualify as a disease.

19th and 20th Centuries

It was not until the 19th Century when rationalism and positivism promoted the belief that man was governed my natural laws and that these laws could be discovered and clarified through science.

Hypothetical versus Symptomatic

In medicine there were major advances in the discovery of bacterial reasons for diseases, such as syphilis, tuberculosis, and typhoid, which sometimes resulted in deviant thinking or behaving. It was reasoned that other such thinking or behaving must be caused by other diseases or for other bodily reasons. Up until the mid-nineteenth century the rationalization behind irrational thinking and behaving was speculative and hypothetical.

The first of two significant changes occurred that initiated a different medical model profile for such irrational thinking and behaving. The first significant change in the medicalization of deviant thinking and behaving resulted from the work of Emil Kraeplin (1856-1926). Kraeplin was a German psychiatrist **who believed that the psychiatric diseases had physical causes and established a classification system of mental disorders**. The classification system involved symptoms that are subjective evidences of disease. Kraeplin considered psychiatry to be a branch of medical science and should be treated as such. Kraeplin's classification system preceded the *Diagnostic and Statistical Manual of Mental Disorders* (*DSM*) and the *International Classification of Diseases* (*ICD*) and certainly influenced them. The *DSM* and *ICD* are predicated on the idea that deviant thinking and behaving are medical issues, i.e., diseases, even though there are no objective biological markers for the disorders listed.

The second significant change was brought about by Sigmund Freud (1856-1939), who is responsible for rapidly advancing the medical model. Instead of moral treatment by means of religion and philosophy, Freud advanced the medical model with its psychological underpinnings. Freud molded his hypothetical psychological themes into a pseudo-scientific framework that propelled them further into medicine. Yet even prior to Freud, deviant thinking and behaving had been quite firmly established as diseases. Under Freud deviant thinking and/or behaving constituted a "disease" and curing such was "medicine." In short, Freud devised a psychotherapy (psychoanalysis) that he represented as a scientific theory and as medical therapy. This was the second significant change in the use of the medical model for mental and behavioral disorders and a significant, unique, and historical precedence-setting act on the part of Freud. This set the standard for future psychotherapies to function without the need for objective biological markers to qualify behaviors as diseases.

Freud is the most prominent name in psychotherapy and is considered the father of the psychotherapy movement. Freud invented psychoanalysis as a method for treating mental-emotional disorders and particularly for investigating what he considered to be the unconscious mind. Psychoanalysis is known as the fountainhead of Western psychotherapy. As such, it has influenced most of contemporary psychotherapy. With Freud's doctrine of the unconscious and its related theories, his work set a standard and framework for others to follow and modify. His ideas permeate later theories and therapies and have significantly influenced the thinking and writing of the twentieth century and beyond. E.M. Thornton says in her book *The Freudian Fallacy*:

> Probably no single individual has had a more profound effect on twentieth-century thought than Sigmund Freud. His works have influenced psychiatry, anthropology, social work, penology, and education and provided a seemingly limitless source of material for novelists and dramatists. Freud has created a "whole new climate of opinion"; for better or worse he has changed the face of society.[7]

Indeed, Freud's constellation of theories about the human psyche is merely a set of one man's fantasies. Regrettably his theories have been elevated from fantasy to fact, accepted as gospel truth, and applied to almost every area of human endeavor. Therefore, it is essential to remember that Freud's ideas and theories are simply unproved opinions, not facts; his own notions, not reality.

In truth, Freud's psychological model and treatment methodology (psychoanalysis) were merely unprovable constructs of his imagination, which became the universal medical model behind all the psychotherapy that followed—absent objective biological proof of disease. Through the malevolent machinations of his mind, Freud brought the psychological into the medical world by giving a scientific-appearing façade to the human mind absent any scientific evidence of disease. And the monstrous acceptance of his scheme, first by the medical community and later by federal funding to universities, became the means of therapizing not only deviant thinking and behaving for veterans at first, but eventually for all problematic thinking and behaving, absent any need to prove that a disease existed. After all, what psychotherapists regard their individual, marital, family clients as having a mental illness? And what psychotherapists show forth objective biological markers for the symptoms of their clients?

Psychotherapy

Szasz asks an important question:

> What is psychotherapy? In the conventional view, it is, generally, the treatment of mental disease—particularly by psychological, social, or environmental, rather than physical or chemical means. In this imagery, psychotherapy is real and objective in the same sense that prescribing peni-

cillin, surgically removing a brain tumor, or setting a fracture are real and objective. Hence we commonly speak of psychiatrists "giving," and patients "receiving," psychotherapy. In my opinion, this view is entirely false.[8]

Szasz later answers that question:

Actually, psychotherapy is a modern, scientific-sounding name for what used to be called the "cure of souls." The true history of psychiatry thus begins not with the early nineteenth-century psychiatrists, but with the Greek philosophers and the Jewish rabbis of antiquity; and it continues with the Catholic priests and Protestant pastors, over a period of nearly two millennia, before the medical soul-doctors appear on the stage of history.[9]

Szasz adds: "The spiritual needs of man were thus well understood in Greek antiquity; and they were well articulated in the religious and artistic images and terms appropriate to them."[10]

Counseling therapy based upon symptoms absent objective biological proof of disease continued to expand through psychiatry. Freud and other such individuals as Carl Jung and Alfred Adler represented popular psychological approaches. However, because these therapies were very intensive and very expensive and because they required meeting 3-5 times a week with a medical doctor, they involved only a small number of individuals who could afford the time and money.

The field of clinical psychology was developed in colleges and universities circa 1950. This relatively new field later produced degreed individuals who would become licensed and enabled to offer a shorter, therefore less expensive, means of dealing with problems of living in the psychiatric tradition of dealing with symptoms without the objective biological evidence of disease, yet depending on the medical model.

After World War II the federal government invested heavily in universities to produce therapists, primarily for returning veterans, never doubting the questionable medical model connection. These additional monies, along with private foundation grants, were used in universities to expand the clinical psychology departments in order to train individuals to conduct therapy. Clinical psychology, out of which come psychotherapists, was a relatively new profession at that time but is now one of the most popular majors in colleges and universities across America.

Ellen Herman, in her book *The Romance of American Psychology*, describes the rise of psychological counseling in America. She says:

> Throughout the entire postwar era, the United States has trained and employed more psychological experts, per capita, than any other country in the world.... Before World War II, professional healers and counselors were few; most individuals allied with psychology did work unrelated to "helping."[11]

Herman describes the omnipresence of psychology as having "seeped into virtually every facet of existence," but she says, "that does not mean that it has always been there or that what experts say has always mattered as much as it matters today."[12]

Dr. Jonathan Engel, in his book *American Therapy: The Rise of Psychotherapy in the United State*, describes the increase in the use of psychotherapy. The dust jacket states:

> Therapy has percolated into the American mind-set—Engel believes there is something uniquely American about the way that we have taken to it as a form of health care and as a kind of self-improvement. Today we are a "counseled nation," where the prescription of antidepressants is widespread and terms like *emotional baggage* are used colloquially. Therapy today reflects the American can-do attitude and it furthers many of our collective goals: emotional well-being, social adjustment, happier marriages, and more productive lives.[13]

In his Preface, Engle makes a significant statement about the uniqueness and ubiquitousness of American psychotherapy. As to its uniqueness, Engel says: "Nowhere else in the world do people explore their deepest and most intimate secrets with total strangers with such alacrity and enthusiasm."[14] As to its ubiquitousness, Engel speaks of the multitude of places and the many reasons and ways that Americans are involved in counseling. It is everywhere!

Aside from individual meetings and brief advice giving, this problem-centered professional counseling mania did not exist in or out of the church prior to World War II. At the same time problem-centered counseling based upon the medical model came in, the bar was lowered as to what constitutes problems that should lead to counseling. The bar was first lowered in society through problem-centered counseling and then some years later the church followed suit. The bar that was lowered was what problems constitute a need for counseling. Whereas, in the past, people were embarrassed and even ashamed about anyone knowing they were in counseling, today seeing a counselor is considered a badge of honor. Clients and counselees in counseling publically reveal not only that they are in counseling, but even say whom they are seeing and what they talk about.

From the Spiritual to the Fleshly

With the rise of affluence after World War II, there was a shift from interest in the supernatural (spiritual) to the natural (fleshly) and from the eternal to the here and now. Instead of seeing the trials and tribulations of life as challenges to faith as a normal part of the Christian experience and even as something to build endurance while looking ahead to a blessed eternity with God, there was an increased desire to seek present happiness through counseling. This also impacted the church where there was a shift from dependence upon God to a dependence upon self to deal with the trials of life. The wisdom of men became the standard of change, and counseling became the means to accomplish happiness here and now. In order to attain here and now happiness, people seek to have the normal twists and trials of life adjusted through problem-centered counseling. Once the objective biological markers were no longer needed to qualify a problem of living for medical insurance coverage, the bar was not just lowered, but practically eliminated when it came to what problems are fair game for the counselor's office.

In her chapter on "The Growth Industry," Herman describes how psychotherapy, absent the need for objective biological markers, grew from treating those with extreme mood disorders to individuals who did not think of themselves as "mentally ill," but wanted what they regarded as the benefits of treatment. Herman concludes her chapter on growth with a section titled "Psychotherapy for the Normal as a Postwar Growth Industry." At the end of it she says:

> Each of the developments described in this chapter expanded psychology's jurisdiction applying the theories and technologies of clinical expertise to more people in more places for more reasons than before.... Strengthening feelings of human connection and identification, struggling to adjust, gain insight, and become fully human— these were gradually transformed into important social goals as well as widespread individual preoccupations during the postwar decades.[15]

Herman later says, "As a result, psychological help [absent the need for objective biological markers] was defined so broadly that everyone needed it."[16] In the last half of the 20th century, the supposed need for psychological counseling and the practice of counseling psychology, rationalized by the medical model, but absent objective biological markers, accelerated rapidly. Instead of having psychoanalysis and its few offshoots, we presently have about 500 different, often conflicting psychological counseling approaches and thousands of not-compatible techniques with various incompatible underlying psychological theories all dependent upon the psychological medical model of mental illness, absent any necessary objective biological markers.

Deviant behaving and thinking first morphed into being called mental illness, absent objective biological markers. Conversation became the treatment for deviant behaving and thinking as it was brought into the field of medicine under the medical model. Later, as the less intensive and less expensive psychotherapies came along, the mental illness/medical model became a façade for counseling problems of living and other mental-emotional-behavioral disorders (absent the needed objective biological markers) instead of or in addition to medicine.

The Public Undressing of Private Lives

"There is a way which seemeth right unto a man, but the end thereof are the ways of death" (Prov. 14:12). Throughout church history the Bible has been sufficient to minister to the personal and interpersonal problems of living without resorting to the very wisdom of man about which God warns His people (1 Cor. 2:5, etc.). How did the church move from the comfort and confidence in the Word of God and the work of the Holy Spirit in the fellowship of the saints to its current condition where solutions to the issues of life are found in the unbiblical evil speaking (Eph. 4:31) that takes place in problem-centered counseling and in the public undressing of private lives? In attempting to provide something better than the world, Christians nevertheless followed the problem-centeredness of worldly counseling along with its sinful speaking. Not only have these Christians opened Pandora's Box, but apparently they believe that its evil contents of exposing the sins and failures of others are necessary in the process of helping people who are suffering from the trials of life. Like the Israelites during the time of the Judges, they are doing what is right in their own eyes (Judges 21:25).

Two main streams of influence occurred historically to promote this evil, both of which began in the secular society and eventually weaseled their way into the church. Like the proverbial camel's nose in the tent, unbiblical evil speaking became the common parlance of God's people. God's Word was first replaced by the "camel" of communication called "counseling," and then Christians went public by expressing instead of suppressing their private emotions, thoughts, and lives. The first stream is counseling, beginning with the psychological counseling movement and followed by the biblical counseling movement, where sinful speaking became part and parcel of the lingua franca of the people of God in the counselor's office. The second and tandem stream is the progression from personal privacy regarding thoughts and lives, once considered sacrosanct and kept private from public disclosure, to public exposure with sinful speaking and its ptomaine touchy-feely talk, with grumps and grumbles rumbling beneath a facile façade of pseudo righteousness. The **publication of private lives first began in the confines of counselors' offices** and eventually evolved into the broadcast blather of talk shows. Jeremiah 17:9 reveals the human depravity from which the sinful problem-centered mania began and is the dreadful abyss of mankind out of which the publicizing of private lives erupted.

The movement in the United States began with private thoughts about self and others being shared in the counseling office and then moved to private lives becoming publicly proclaimed with many defamed. Both of these streams set the stage for counseling conversations running roughshod over the "faith which was once delivered unto the saints" (Jude 3) and ignoring biblical admonitions regarding the tongue (James 3).

Publicizing Private Lives

Once upon a time there was no licensed problem-centered counseling as we know it today, except for psychoanalysis. There were no degreed and licensed counselors who charged money for ongoing conversations about the issues of life. That was sixty years ago. Now this sinful problem-centered counseling has become so much a part of our culture that speaking out against it, as we do, raises eyebrows and hackles. However, the problem we have with counseling is that it is problem-centered and inevitably leads to sinful speaking.

Problem-centered counseling attempts to deal with personal and relational troubles, difficulties, and dilemmas normally taken to a psychological or biblical counselor and discussed in detail and at length with the counselor. They are the mental-emotional-behavioral problems of living that are normally surfaced in counseling and constitute the center of the conversation. Although counselees generally come in with a problem-centered mind-set, the counselors are the ones who are primarily responsible for the corrupt counseling conversations that follow, through their questions and responses.

Problem-centered counseling **is not** like a Catholic confessional in which a person comes alone as a penitent, sorrowful about some sin or wrongdoing on one's own part and seeking forgiveness.[17] Note the person (penitent) is confessing one's own sin and not that of others. Contrary to the Catholic confessional, problem-centered counseling generally flows in the opposite direction in that the client or counselee is typically confessing sins of others who are usually not present, thus making public to a third party what was formerly private and at the same time violating biblical admonitions to the contrary. The Catholic confessional does not consist of repeated meetings about problems with on-going discussions comprised of confessing the sins of others, unbiblically accusing and blaming them, and publicizing their personal and private lives. Repentant sinners who confess their own sins without excuse or blame, rather than the sins of others, are the exception in biblical counseling. While in many instances it would be beneficial if the one in need would first confess one's own sins before discussing the reason for seeking help, it is unlikely to happen because we live in a 2 Timothy 3, last-days era. At least it has not happened in the biblical counseling we have seen, heard, and read. And, it has not happened in almost forty years of our own ministry to others.

Conversations between and among people have been going on ever since the Garden of Eden. Conversation is the sharing of thoughts, feelings, and ideas by spoken communication and includes both informal and formal sharing of words. The kind of conversation to which we are referring is both. It will sound informal and casual at times. It is formal in that it is the kind of conversation that occurs when one or more persons with a personal or interpersonal problem come to a particular person known as a counselor or psychotherapist in order to receive help. The help is given within the formal framework of the counselor's particular theory, techniques, and training. But the backdrop is that the counselee generally reveals confidences and confesses sins of others. The counselor enables the counselee to do so through particular learned theories and techniques, which generally expand the confidences revealed, but fail to find out the truth behind what is said. When one crosses the line from confessing one's own sins to confessing the sins of others, the fleshly tendency in such a setting will inevitably turn to revealing confidences and private matters resulting in speaking evil of others. The depravity of one's flesh generally takes over in such a problem-centered setting.

This publicizing of private lives is umbilically tied to the psychologizing of the American public and began primarily by corrupting the strengths and virtues of women as a conduit through which private lives became publicly exposed and emotively displayed. Janice Peck, in her book *The Age of Oprah: Cultural Icon for the Neoliberal Era*, says:

> Epstein and Steinberg suggest that therapy, as a "language of self and interpersonal relationships, and even as a way of life," had become so pervasive in late-twentieth-century American culture "that it is virtually impossible to live in the United States without being interpolated into the therapeutic experience in some way."[18]

These kinds of talk shows should be renamed as "therapy talk shows" because that is what they are. Such talk show conversations, almost regardless of the topic, are framed in the psychotherapeutic ethos of the current culture.

The United States has privately and publicly become a therapeutic society, where private and public trash talk, which was first led by men counselors and later mainly by women counselors, was primarily fueled by female inclinations and interests. These new private and public personas for women have overshadowed traditional women's roles. Men are being cajoled or cudgeled into the counselor's office in greater numbers than ever before, and in the process they are being brainwashed to think womanly thoughts and to learn that, to save their marriages and salvage their other relationships, they "have to become a woman."[19] If women were not in counseling as counselees, the men would not be there and the whole counseling mania would disintegrate. As to the public puffery of the privacy of personal lives by women, men were later enticed to join the melee of media voices, but to this day the public undressing of private lives is female friendly territory and a dysfunctional environment for traditional men. However, the online era has dramatically expanded such therapeutic interchanges to include men in the social networking and the public exposure of private lives and appears to be the penultimate era prior to the Lord's return. While these streams of discourse have seriously affected the church, we will primarily pursue the curse of problem-centered counseling and the reasons why it should be stopped.

Self-Centeredness

Psychological counseling and its penchant for sinful speaking is a Western phenomenon that has been copied by those in the biblical counseling movement. In her book *In Therapy We Trust: America's Obsession for Self-Fulfillment*, Eva Moskowitz reveals the contrast between "Americans' proclivity for the couch" and other contrasting nations world-wide. She says:

> Though we recognize the therapeutic gospel's grip on our culture, we have little idea how we came to this point. Perhaps this is because the therapeutic has snuck up on us. Perhaps it is because we are only dimly aware that America has not always been obsessed with the psyche. But our therapeutic faith is neither timeless nor universal. Our nation has not always been so preoccupied with personal dilemmas and emotional cures, nor are other nations so preoccupied today. The citizens of Asia, Africa, and Europe do not share Americans' proclivity for the couch. There are fewer psychological professionals in China, Israel, and Korea combined, for example, than there are sex and art therapists in America.[20]

Dr. Frank Furedi, a professor of sociology at the University of Kent, reports in his book *Therapy Culture*:

> A study of "seeker churches" in the US argues that their ability to attract new recruits is based on their ability to tap into the therapeutic understanding of Americans.[21]

Although corrupt-talk counseling is a Western activity, other countries are beginning to adopt it because of

Western influence. While it is on the increase, there has been little of this counseling in East Asian countries. One major reason it is almost non-existent there is because East Asians have typically **not** been **self-oriented** or personal problem-centered. They have typically been **we-oriented**, while Westerners are typically **me-centered**. Also, the culture and tradition of East Asians has been to regard the family as sacred. Therefore one would not blame family or parents for one's present life.

One specialist writing on "psychotherapy in Japan" refers to the "family's sacrosanct character" and the reluctance to blame "a parent or parent's role in a patient's neurosis or, especially, the ways in which a maternal figure may not be all-loving and good." The article says, "A Japanese, instead of investigating his past, romanticizes it: Instead of analyzing his early childhood, he creates fictions about it." The contrast to Western individualism is seen in the following: "Even for [Japanese] adults, expressions of individuality are often considered signs of selfish immaturity."[22]

One writer describes the East/West cleavage this way:

> The world can be divided in many ways—rich and poor, democratic and the authoritarian—but one of the most striking is the divide between the societies with an individualist mentality and the ones with a collectivist mentality....
>
> You can create a global continuum with the most individualistic societies—like the United States or Britain—on one end, and the most collectivist societies—like China or Japan—on the other.[23]

Many Latin American cultures also represent a contrast to the Western "me" culture. While there are some regional differences, Latin American cultures are generally "we" cultures. Mexican writer Octavio Paz describes this tendency:

> I am another when I am, my actions are more mine if they are also everyone's. So that I can exist I must be the other, I must leave myself to look for myself among the others, those who would not exist if I did not, those who give me my own existence. I am not, there is no I, **always it is we**.[24] (Bold added.)

In comparing the aspect of collectivism/individualism between Spanish Speaking South Americans (SSSAs) and English Speaking North Americans (ESNAs), Skye Stephenson says that for SSSAs, "the opinions of others are often given significant weight in evaluating personal behavior and deciding upon appropriate actions" and that the "focus on others' opinions, especially for self-evaluation, is encouraged in most SSSAs from a very young age" and is shown in the way children are scolded.[25] SSSAs are encouraged not to shame the group, while, in contrast, ESNAs are encouraged to follow their own personal beliefs.

Geert and Gert Jan Hofstede describe collectivism, in contrast to individualism, as "societies in which people from birth onward are integrated into strong, cohesive in-groups, which throughout people's lifetimes continue to protect them in exchange for unquestioning loyalty."[26] They say that "in a collectivist environment" family and group ties are very strong, "it is immoral *not* to treat one's in-group members better than others," and shaming is used to correct bad behavior because it makes the family or group look bad"[27] (italics theirs). So we see a similarity to East Asian culture in many Latin American cultures where the group and family are sacred and where focusing on the self and condemning the group or family are discouraged. Without North American influence, such Latin American cultures are **not** naturally fertile territory for psychotherapy and counseling.

Cure of Souls (Spiritual Model) or Cure of Minds (Medical Model)?

From the very beginning of the Christian church there was a method and a ministry for dealing with mental-emotional problems. The method depended upon the Word of God, which describes both the condition of man and the process of relief for troubled minds. The ministry was a prayer and healing ministry which dealt with all nonorganic mental-emotional disturbances. This entire process was known as the "cure of souls." John T. McNeill in A *History of the Cure of Souls* describes this ministry as "the sustaining and curative treatment of persons in those matters that reach beyond the requirements of the animal life."[28]

Sin or Sickness?

Whereas the church once believed in, spoke of, and practiced the cure of souls, it has shifted its faith to a secular cure of minds. Szasz very ably describes how this change came about: "With the soul securely displaced by the mind and the mind securely subsumed as a function of the brain—people speak of the 'cure of minds.'"[29] The brain is a physical organ; the mind is not. With this subtle semantic twist, the mind (disguised as an organ of the body) was falsely elevated as a scientific and medical concept in contrast to the soul, which is a theological idea. A choice was made between a so-called scientific concept and a theological one. The average person does not see that both mind and soul are abstract concepts. One is an abstraction of psychotherapy and the other is an abstraction of religion. Neither the mind nor the soul can be discovered through medical or scientific means.

At the same time as a physical organ (the brain) was confused with an abstraction (the mind), another change took place. Whereas the church had believed that there was a relationship of sin and circumstances in many mental-emotional disorders, the psychotherapist introduced the medical concept of sickness, absent objective biological markers, to explain such disorders. Nevertheless, mental suffering itself is not synonymous with sickness; it is a symptom. Mental suffering may be a primary symptom, but it is not sickness itself. We have only been deluded into thinking that it is. We easily accepted the word *sickness* to refer to mental-emotional problems because that was the "loving" and "understanding" way to cover up moral responsibility—ours as well as theirs.

One of Szasz's main purposes in writing *The Myth of Psychotherapy* was this:

> I shall try to show how, with the decline of religion and the growth of science in the eighteenth century, the cure of (sinful) souls, which had been an integral part of the Christian religions, was recast as the cure of (sick) minds, and became an integral part of medical science.[30]

The words *sinful* and *sick* in parentheses are his. These two words mark the dramatic shift from the cure of souls to the cure of minds.

There is a serious problem when people confuse passion with tissue and sin with sickness. Such confusion of words leads to erroneous thinking. And this very confusion and error virtually ended the cure of souls ministry in the church. Through a semantic trick, the mind was confused with the brain and the misnomer of sickness replaced the concept of sin. And the entire subjective, theoretical process of psychotherapy ensconced itself safely in the realm of science and medicine under the guise of the medical model. But, in reality, psychotherapy is a misfit as medicine and an impostor as science.

The recipe was simple. Replace the cure of souls with the cure of minds by confusing an abstraction (mind) with a biological organ (brain), and thus convince people that mental healing and medical healing are the same. Stir in a dash of theory disguised as fact. Call it all science and put it into medicine and the rest is history. The medical model that justified psychoanalysis was no longer needed as the later psychotherapies, following psychoanalysis, were developed. The new psychotherapies no longer needed the medical model to support their existence and use. With the rise of psychotherapy, there was a decline in the pastoral cure of souls. Secular psychotherapy has taken over to such an extent that Szasz says, "Actually, psychotherapy is a modern, scientific-sounding name for what used to be called the 'cure of souls.'"[31] Thus we have the shell without the power, without the life, and without the Lord.

Christianity is more than a belief system or a theological creed. Christianity is not just what happens in church. Christianity is faith in a living Lord and in His indwelling Holy Spirit. Christianity involves the entire life: every day, every action, every decision, every thought, every emotion. One cannot adequately treat an individual apart from this life force. Nor can we segment the mental and emotional from the belief system of a person. For too long we have looked to the church to answer our theological questions and looked elsewhere for answers to our life problems. Christians who have God's Holy Spirit living in them are spiritual beings; therefore they need spiritual answers to life's dilemmas.

It is understandable that the world would reject the Living Water of the Word of God in seeking to understand and help individuals suffering from mental-emotional-behavioral problems. However, as the world rejected the biblical answers, the church began to doubt its own doctrine of sin, salvation, and sanctification in relation to mental-emotional-behavioral issues. Many ministers even left their pastorates to become licensed psychotherapists.

We maintain that God and His Word provide a completely sufficient foundation for living the Christian life, which would include mental-emotional-behavioral soundness. We further maintain that the Bible contains the healing balm for all nonorganically-based problems of living that might be labeled as mental-emotional-behavioral disorders. The Bible should also be used to minister encouragement in the Lord to the souls of those who are suffering from biological diseases, even when they are under the care of a medical doctor.

Conclusion

As we have shown, religion was previously the main way of dealing with the issues of life, including deviant thinking and behaving, but gradually the medical model, absent objective biological markers, eclipsed the biblical model and mutated into a psychological model. Szasz clearly states, "I regard psychotherapy as a moral rather than a medical enterprise."[32] He also says: "In ancient Israel and Greece the healer of the soul is thus not the physician but the rabbi and the philosopher."[33] In his chapter on "Origins of the Medical Model," Torrey says:

> It has taken medicine over 3,000 years to seize the province of irrational behavior from the fiefdoms of law, religion, and philosophy; once seized there was an obligation to protect it against non-medical usurpers.[34]

As we have shown in detail elsewhere, psychotherapy is religion and is truly pseudoscience and, therefore a pseudo-medical practice.[35] The significance of psychotherapy being religion and pseudoscience is that this religious pseudoscience has replaced the cure of souls throughout many areas of the church, including Christian schools, colleges, universities, seminaries, denominations, and mission agencies.

2

The *DSM* and "Mental Illness"

According to research psychiatrist E. Fuller Torrey, "The vast majority of people whom we call 'mentally ill' have problems of living rather than physical disabilities. They are not 'sick.'"[1] In other words, there are numerous irrational behavior and thinking symptoms that individuals experience and exhibit that should **not** be labelled *mental illness*, **because they do not have objective biological evidence of disease.**

The medical model of deviant human thinking and behaving is based on the idea that there is a biological reason for each deviant thought or behavior. In other words, the roots of deviant thinking and behaving are considered to be biological. The medical model is often expressed through the metaphor *mental illness*. The use of the term *mental illness* presumes that there is some biological reason behind the thinking and behaving (medical model) even when no objective biological markers are found.

We reveal why the use of the generally accepted medical model of deviant human thinking and behaving

41

is scientifically dysfunctional. We shall demonstrate how prolifically acceptable the application to aberrant human thinking and behaving the medical model has become and how scientifically errant it is, both in diagnosis and treatment.

The *Diagnostic and Statistical Manual of Mental Disorders* (*DSM*) is based on the medical model of mental illness. It describes and categorizes mental-emotional-behavioral symptoms for the purposes of diagnosis and treatment. From Hippocrates' time to the present, numerous labels for such symptoms have been proposed. However, as we said earlier, the use of such labels became more systematized around the beginning of the last century. Emil Kraeplin, a contemporary of Sigmund Freud, developed a classification system, which eventually led to the present *DSM* system used by psychiatrists. The American Psychiatric Association published the *DSM* and psychiatrists regard the *Manual* as the bible of mental disorders, in spite of the fact that it is a subjective instrument based on subjective symptoms rather than on objective biological evidence. According to the American Psychiatric Association, the *DSM* is:

> … the handbook used by health care professionals in the United States and much of the world as the authoritative guide to the diagnosis of mental disorders. *DSM* contains descriptions, symptoms, and other criteria for diagnosing mental disorders.[2]

The first edition of the *DSM* was published in 1952. After several later versions the most recent version, *DSM*-5, was published in 2013. Whereas the first edition had 145 pages and weighed 12.6 ounces, the *DSM-5* has 991 pages and weighs 3.4 pounds!

Nearly all these mental disorders are based upon subjective reports by the clients, because there are no obvious or clear organic, physical origins to support the diagnoses. The University of California *Berkeley Wellness Letter* reports:

> Mental illness is both extremely common... and extremely hard to diagnose in some cases, since no simple biological tests exist to detect them. There's no blood test for, say, depression or a personality disorder; no scan that can reveal attention-deficit hyperactivity disorder (ADHD). Instead, a clinician must rely solely on a patient's symptoms and observation of his or her behavior to reach a diagnosis.[3]

Dr. Jeffrey Lieberman, having served as chairman of psychiatry at Columbia University and president of the American Psychiatric Association, says: "With rare exceptions such as narcolepsy, which can be diagnosed by testing cerebrospinal fluid, there are no objective biological measures for mental illness."[4]

Think of the implications of having **"no objective biological measures for mental illness"** for the nearly 300 mental disorders in the *DSM-5*. All of the *DSM* disorders (also called *illnesses* or *diseases*) have symptoms, but, except for narcolepsy, they lack objective biological markers to qualify as diseases. **All of the *DSM* disorders are dependent upon the medical model** with the assumption that all the underlying biological causes will eventually be found.

Those who hold to the medical model of mental illness may justify the use of the metaphor *illness* by saying they mean brain diseases and speak in terms of the structure and function of the brain being impaired. In response to that idea, Torrey says:

> There are many known diseases of the brain, with changes in both structure and function. Tumors, multiple sclerosis, meningitis, and neurosyphilis are some examples. But these diseases are considered to be in the province of neurology rather than of psychiatry. And the demarcation between the two is sharp.[5]

It is presumed that causes will eventually be identified for many of the conditions now labeled *mental illness* or *mental disorder* as has been identified for narcolepsy. However, as we just indicated, only one of the nearly 300 mental disorders listed in the DSM has a clearly established causal objective biological marker. In other words, no structural or functional changes in the brain have been confirmed for the others.

Human Complexity

King David, astounded by the amazing way God created us, exclaimed: "I will praise thee; for I am fearfully and wonderfully made: marvelous are thy works; and that my soul knoweth right well" (Ps. 139:14). By inspiration he wrote about our genetic make-up hidden within the coded language of the DNA:

> My substance was not hid from thee, when I was made in secret, and curiously wrought in the lowest parts of the earth. Thine eyes did see my sub-

stance, yet being unperfect [unfulfilled]; and in thy book **all my members were written**, which in continuance were fashioned, when as yet there was none of them (Ps. 139: 15-16, bold added).

Every human being starts out with a complex set of DNA, which has been affected by the fall to the extent that individuals may be genetically vulnerable to certain diseases. Today scientists are finding certain patterns that may predict disease vulnerability. For instance, Huntington's Disease often has mental symptoms of anxiety, apathy, depression, moodiness, irritability, aggression, and psychosis, some of which may precede the physical symptoms.[6]

Yes, we are "fearfully and wonderfully made" and scientists have just touched the surface! The brain itself is considered the "last frontier of medicine," and the more that is discovered, the greater the realization that much remains a mystery. The brain interacts with every part of the body as well as with the external environment, and now scientists have revealed that it also interacts with the vast number of microbes in the intestine.

The Human Brain

Adding to the complicated conundrum of no objective biological markers for all but one of the nearly 300 DSM disorders is the complexity of the human brain. An article in the *Psychotherapy Networker* describes the human brain as "the most complex biological entity known on earth." The author adds, "The number of possible interconnections among its neurons exceeds the estimated number of atoms in the universe."[7] Christof Koch declares, "The brain is by far the most complex piece of highly excitable matter in the known universe by any measure. We don't even understand the brain of a worm."[8] An article in *Psychology Today* reports that there are "100 billion neurons in the human brain" and that it would take 32 million years "to count each synapse in the human brain at a rate of one synapse per second."[9] Dr. Stephen Smith, a professor of molecular and cellular physiology says:

> One synapse, by itself, is more like a microprocessor—with both memory-storage and information-processing elements—than a mere on/off switch. In fact, one synapse may contain on the order of 1,000 molecular-scale switches. A single human brain has more switches than all the computers and routers and Internet connections on Earth.[10]

David Cloud reports:

> The brain receives signals from 137 million light receptors in the eyes, 100,000 hearing receptors in the ears, 10,000 taste buds, 5-6 million odor detecting cells, 30,000 heat sensors on the skin, 250,000 cold sensors, and 500,000 touch sensors (adapted from Bert Thompson, *The Revelation of God and Nature*). The hearing receptors alone send up to 25,000 auditory signals per second to the brain, which interprets them as voices, thunder, music, or a million other sounds (Jackson, *The Human Body*).[11]

Torrey reveals:

There are chemical and neurological components to *all* activities of the brain. Each thought, wish, memory, or impulse has a chemical or neurological component.[12] (Italics in original.)

The brain is obviously central to the mind-body relationship because it **controls** each of the 79 organ systems in the body. In addition, the brain also **responds** to every organ system within the body.[13] This interaction of body to brain/mind and brain/ mind to body is a complex process, and the enigma of it prevents us from knowing much truth about the underlying causes of mental symptoms. Knowledge is limited because the secrets of human behavior are locked up in the brain-mind-body relationship. Michael Chase, in an article entitled "The Matriculating Brain," wrote:

The human brain, for all our intimacy with it, has surrendered less to scientific research than have the distant moon, stars and ocean floor, or such intimate processes as genetic coding, immune reactions or muscle contraction.[14]

In his book *The Mind-Gut Connection*, University of California, Los Angeles professor and researcher Dr. Emeran Mayer tells us that "there are 100,000 times more microbes in your gut alone as there are people on earth."[15] Throughout his book Mayer describes how this huge population can influence the brain in various ways. He describes how the gut and brain interact and how the gut microbe population can influence health and, if disturbed, "may even play a role in autism spectrum disorders and neuro-degenerative brain disorders like Parkinson's disease."[16] He says:

> Your gut microbes are engaged in ongoing conversations with your GI tract, your immune system, your enteric nervous system, and your brain—and as with any cooperative relationship, healthy communication is essential. Recent research reveals that the disturbance of these conversations can lead to GI diseases, including inflammatory bowel disease and antibiotic-associated diarrhea, and obesity, with all its deleterious consequences, and may be involved in development of many serious brain diseases, including depression, Alzheimer's disease, and autism.[17]

Numerous articles can be found on government and educational websites on the "Gut-Brain Axis." The Abstract for one article, in giving an overview of the influence of the gut on feelings and behavior, says:

> The gut-brain axis (GBA) consists of bidirectional communication between the central and the enteric nervous system, linking emotional and cognitive centers of the brain with peripheral intestinal functions. Recent advances in research have described the importance of gut microbiota in influencing these interactions.[18]

In an article from *Trends in Neuroscience* titled "Gut-brain axis: how the microbiome influences anxiety and depression," Jane A. Foster and Karen-Anne McVey Neufeld say:

> Going forward, there is a significant opportunity to consider how the gut–brain axis and, in particular, new tools will allow researchers to under-

stand how dysbiosis [imbalance] of the microbiome influences mental illness.[19]

This entire field of research into the Gut-Brain Axis is fairly new and much has yet to be discovered regarding how people can be helped. However, this is one more example of how complex we are and, therefore, why proper diagnosis is so very vital, particularly in how the gut affects the brain and how the brain affects the mind. In other words, instead of thinking "It's all in your head," perhaps it's all in your gut. Or, instead of it being a psychological problem, it is a biological problem needing a biological solution. Or, instead of it being solely a spiritual problem, it is indeed a biological problem affecting the brain and thereby affecting the mind, will, and emotions. Or, instead of it being a psychological or biological problem, it may be a spiritual problem after all.

Context of Symptoms

Symptoms of fear and depression are often simply normal responses to life's challenges. Therefore, one also must add context to the confusing mixture of influences on the mind and issues of the soul. Not everything is biological and not everything is abnormal. The context in which symptoms occur is extremely important, particularly when it comes to fear, anxiety, and depression. For instance, fear is a natural response when confronting a bear or a rabid dog or even if there is an unusual noise in the house. Sadness is an appropriate and normal response to disappointment or loss. Frustration can be entirely normal under many circumstances. Anxiety is also a normal response to fearful events, such as public speaking. There is often too hasty a diagnosis when a behavior should be recognized as normal within the surrounding circumstances.

In the forward to a book titled *Loss of Sadness: How Psychiatry Transformed Normal Sorrow into Depressive Disorder*, Robert Spitzer says:

> *The Loss of Sadness* represents the most cogent and compelling "inside" challenge to date to the diagnostic revolution that began almost 30 years ago in the field of psychiatry. The authors begin by arguing for the existence of a universal intuitive understanding that to be human means to naturally react with feelings of sadness to negative events in one's life. In contrast, when the symptoms of sadness (e.g., sad feelings, difficulty sleeping, inability to concentrate, reduced appetite) have no apparent cause or are grossly disproportionate to the apparent cause, the intuitive understanding is that something important in human functioning has gone wrong, indicating the presence of a depressive disorder. Horwitz and Wakefield then persuasively argue, as the book's central thesis, that contemporary psychiatry confuses normal sadness with depressive mental disorder because it ignores the relationship of symptoms to the context in which they emerge. The psychiatric diagnosis of Major Depression is based on the assumption that symptoms alone can indicate that there is a disorder; this assumption allows normal responses to stressors to be mischaracterized as symptoms of disorder. The authors demonstrate that this confusion has im-

portant implications not only for psychiatry and its patients but also for society in general.[20]

This foreword by Spitzer is especially telling since he was involved in creating the third edition of the *Diagnostic & Statistical Manual of Mental Disorders* in 1980. Since then he has been concerned about clinicians diagnosing according to symptoms alone without considering the context in which emotional or behavioral symptoms occur.

What happens when a true disease is found? Torrey makes and elaborates on a very important point that mostly explains the need for what he titled his book: *The Death of Psychiatry*. He says:

> Furthermore, one of the hallmarks of psychiatry has been that each time causes were found for mental "diseases," the conditions were taken away from psychiatry and reassigned to other specialties. As the mental "diseases" were shown to be true diseases, mongolism and phenylketonuria were assigned to pediatrics; epilepsy and neurosyphilis became the concerns of neurology; and delirium due to infectious diseases was handled by internists. In some cases, they have remained part of the psychiatric classificatory system, but in fact, the actual care of the disease has been transferred elsewhere. **One is left with the impression that psychiatry is the repository for all suspected brain "diseases" for which there is no known cause.**[21] (Bold added.)

Torrey clarifies: "Diseases are something we *have*, behavior is something we *do* (italics in original)."[22] On this premise, Torrey develops his theory that the majority of people whom we call "mentally ill" have problems of living rather than physical disabilities.

It is reported that:

> Critics, including the National Institute of Mental Health, argue that the *DSM* represents an unscientific and subjective system. There are ongoing issues concerning the validity and reliability of the diagnostic categories; the reliance on superficial symptoms; the use of artificial dividing lines between categories and from "normality"; possible cultural bias; and medicalization of human distress.[23]

Someone has suggested that the American Psychiatric Association would like to have one mental disorder label for each American or at least enough labels to cover the total population. Jay Katz, a professor of psychiatry at Yale, admitted under oath in court testimony, "If you look at [the *DSM*] you can classify all of us under one rubric or another of mental disorder."[24] Psychiatrist Jonas Robitscher says that "some psychiatrists have raised the estimate of the incidence of neurosis in our society to 95 percent or more."[25]

The whole classification scheme is a blatant testimony to the questionability of mental illnesses and the unscientific nature of psychotherapy. The American Psychiatric Association's *DSM* excludes those conditions which "have strong cultural or subcultural supports or sanctions."[26] These criteria were used in this classification scheme to keep homosexuality off the list of diseases. However, these criteria were not uniformly applied to all forms of behavior.

The lopsidedness of the scheme is apparent in that "caffeine intoxication" and "caffeine withdrawal" are now mental diseases along with "alcohol use disorder,"[27] but not all pedophiles have a mental disorder.[28] To further compound the ludicrousness of the ritual of psychic labeling, the *Comprehensive Textbook* says that its definition of *mental disorder* "may need to be changed in future years to correspond with a change in the attitude of society and the psychiatric profession toward certain conditions.".[29].

It is a strange disease that is determined by personal distress, cultural acceptability, and changing attitudes. In the biological sphere a disease is a disease regardless of personal distress or cultural acceptability. Dr. Margaret Hagen, in her book *Whores of the Court*, describes the ubiquitous use of the *DSM* and how necessary it is to be able to bill and receive payments from third-party providers.[30]

> If you are not Pollyanna-happy—and complain loudly about the fact that you are not—the odds are great that a psychoexpert can and will diagnose a mental problem for you.

> Once society has accepted that the hundreds of ways people can be unhappy can all be labeled as specific mental disorders, then the diagnosis of those states of unhappiness, those disorders, becomes the special province of mental disorder experts.[31]

It is no wonder that the subtitle of Hagan's books is *The Fraud of Psychiatric Testimony and the Rape of American Justice*!

Psychiatrist Irwin Savodnik's article "Psychiatry's sick compulsion: turning weakness into diseases" in the *Los Angeles Times* targets the *DSM* and the American Psychiatric Association. Savodnik says:

> The association [APA] specializes in turning ordinary human frailty into disease…. The association has been inventing mental illnesses for the last 50 years or so. The original diagnostic manual appeared in 1952 and contained 107 diagnoses and 132 pages, by my count. [32]

Reuters reports that the current *Diagnostic and Statistical Manual of Mental Disorders* (*DSM*) is over 900 pages and contains nearly "300 maladies (from 'dependent personality disorder' and 'voyeuristic disorder' to 'delayed ejaculation,' 'kleptomania' and 'intermittent explosive disorder'), each limning [portraying] the potential woes of being human." [33] Savodnik comments on the explosion of maladies added since the *DSM I*. He says;

> Nowhere in the rest of medicine has such a proliferation of categories occurred. The reason for this difference between psychiatry and other medical specialties has more to do with ideology than with science. [34]

Paul Genova, an associate professor of psychiatry at the University of Vermont, made the following remarks in the *Psychiatric Times* in an article titled "Dump the *DSM*!":

The American Psychiatric Association's *DSM* diagnostic system has outlived its usefulness by about two decades. It should be abandoned, not revised ... it is time for the arbitrary, legalistic symptom checklists of the *DSM* to go ... the aggregate is an awkward, ponderous, off-putting beast that discredits and diminishes psychiatry and the insight of those who practice it.

Consider the fact that your clinical practice is governed by a diagnostic system that:

• is a laughingstock for the other medical specialties;

• requires continual apologies to primary care doctors, medical students, residents, and the occasional lawyer or judge;

• most of our thoughtful colleagues privately rail against;

• insists upon rigid categories that often serve only to confuse and misinform patients and their clinical workers (sometimes abetted by televised drug advertising);

• is so intellectually incoherent as to raise eyebrows among the well-educated, critical thinkers in our own psychotherapy clientele;

• persuades the world at large that psychiatry no longer has anything of interest to say about the human condition.

> If it were within your power to do so, wouldn't
> you get rid of this system?[35]

What we have here is a disastrous Pandora's Box. The definition of Pandora's Box is "a process that generates many complicated problems as the result of unwise inference in something." [36] The fact that, with one exception, there are no objective biological markers for the nearly 300 *DSM* disorders opens Pandora's Box to "many complicated problems" which influence a Christian response to mental illness.

After all is said about diseases, the relationship between the mind and the gut, and the context of symptoms, we must remember that God created humans with a soul and a conscience. Therefore, within the context of the Bible and all that is included in the spiritual life, we must consider God's involvement in every aspect of our being. Fear may originate in the conscience; sadness may come from the consciousness of sin in oneself and others. God created people with emotions and the Bible has much to say about emotional issues. In fact, some symptoms may come from alienation from God. Christ calls individuals to come to Him to find rest and peace:

> Come unto me, all *ye* that labour and are heavy laden, and I will give you rest. Take my yoke upon you, and learn of me; for I am meek and lowly in heart: and ye shall find rest unto your souls. For my yoke *is* easy, and my burden is light. (Matt. 11:28-30.)

3

Misdiagnosis and Maltreatment

One of the most difficult issues to deal with is the cause and treatment of mental-emotional-behavioral disorders. There are hundreds of varieties of such disorders with the more popularly known ones being depression, anxiety, bipolar disorder, and schizophrenia. The big question is whether such brain disorders are biological, spiritual, or a combination of the two. We begin with the axiom that the brain is both a biological and at the same time a spiritual entity.

The intimate relationship between the brain/body and the mind has led to much misunderstanding and misdiagnosing during the entire history of psychiatry and psychotherapy. The problem of biological disorders that were thought to be psychological problems and treated as such is a grim skeleton in the therapeutic closet. Many psychiatrists would like to ignore or forget about this history of looking at and treating mental-emotional-behavioral symptoms that were really the result of physical diseases not identified at the time.

At one time in this history there were undetected physical diseases which were treated as mental disorders because of the accompanying mental symptoms, and it is still true today. Two examples are general paresis, caused by the spirochete of syphilis invading the brain, and pellagrous psychosis, caused by a dietary deficiency of nicotinic acid. In both cases numerous people who have suffered from these diseases were labeled *schizophrenic* and treated accordingly. The following account is just one of many case histories involving misdiagnosis.

A twenty-two-year-old woman exhibited certain symptoms similar to those of schizophrenia. Rather than suggesting a comprehensive physical, the psychiatrist to whom she was referred diagnosed her condition as schizophrenia and treated her accordingly. However, it was later discovered that her depression and hallucinations were due to pellagrous psychosis, which had been brought on by a crash diet and near starvation conditions.

Treating such a person with psychotherapy or psychotropic medication instead of treating the physical problem not only prevents possible cure, but also adds even more horror to the agony of the disease itself. Can you imagine how many people have suffered from such physical diseases and have been treated as having a mental disorder because of ignorance of the real problem? Even Parkinson's disease was once considered a mental disorder and treated by means of psychotherapy. Another example is that of peptic ulcer disease (PUD). Doctors were trained to believe and told patients that the cause of PUD was mental (stress). The accepted treatment for PUD was a bland diet plus antacids plus counseling to reduce the stress. Then in 1984, physicians Robin Warren and Barry Marshall from Australia claimed that PUD was not caused merely by overproduction of gastric acid as a result of stress, but by a specific bacterium, *Helicobacter pylori.* So, the solution was not diet, antacids and counseling, but rather antibiotics.[1]

This raises the whole problem of misdiagnosis and the tendency to refer people to psychiatry or psychotherapy. There have been and still are great numbers of individuals erroneously referred to psychiatry and psychotherapy who are really suffering from physical disorders. Sydney Walker III, a neuropsychiatrist, says:

> Each year, hundreds of thousands of Americans who are actually suffering from common medical conditions such as hyperthyroidism, Lyme disease, and even poor nutrition are misdiagnosed with psychiatric disorders. Studies show that the rate of misdiagnosis is more than 4 in 10.[2]

There is a whole range of bodily disorders that have mental-emotional, behavioral symptoms. Some of these biological disorders are in their embryonic stages—not yet detectable. These symptoms can result in personal discomfort and interpersonal problems.

A number of people, whose neurotic and psychotic behavior has been caused by low blood sugar, have been treated by psychotherapy because the disorder was not recognized as hypoglycemia. One twenty-six-year-old woman suffered from symptoms of depression and anxiety. For an entire year, she had been taking tranquilizers and seeing a psychotherapist on a regular basis before a doctor properly diagnosed her condition as hypoglycemia. Furthermore, she had been hospitalized twice because of persistent suicidal thoughts.[3]

Dr. Allen Bergin, in his article "Psychotherapy Can Be Dangerous," mentions a female patient who had several physical problems and was being treated by a psychotherapist. He reports, "Although he had an M.D., he never suggested a physical examination. A subsequent medical exam revealed she was suffering from anemia and low metabolism."[4]

Another example of misdiagnosis, maltreatment, and the accompanying nightmare is found in neurosurgeon I. S. Cooper's book *The Victim Is Always the Same*.[5] One of the most pathetic parts of the book has to do with two little girls who had the rare disease dystonia, which is a neurological disease involving involuntary muscular movements mainly of the arms and legs. Before it was finally discovered that they were actually suffering from dystonia, the girls and their parents went through almost endless psychotherapy, all in the name of diagnosis, treatment, and help.

All the doctors and social workers involved thought only of psychological factors as they observed the overt symptoms, which consisted of strange movements while walking and odd, disconnected arm movements. The professionals regarded these symptoms as bizarre behavior, which they felt indicated that the girls were emotionally disturbed and were symbolically acting out inner struggle and anxiety. Through the various interviews, the parents were regarded as neurotic, distressed, and anxious. No one evidently stopped to consider that these parents were naturally concerned about their children and the diagnoses they were hearing.

Both parents and girls underwent weeks and months of individual and group psychotherapy. One of the girls was even admitted to a psychiatric hospital. The more the symptoms persisted, the more the professionals told the parents that they were not cooperating and that there was resistance to therapy. One child went through the agony of being interviewed in front of television cameras and in front of other doctors and, worst of all, she was not allowed to see her parents, who, it was thought, might ruin the therapy with their own presence.

At last, quite by accident, one of the neurologists in the hospital happened to notice the child in passing and identified what she had—a disease called dystonia. Throughout this entire period of time, Cooper reports, the psychiatrists, psychologists, social workers, and group therapists demonstrated an astonishing amount of self-confidence in what they were doing. One might wonder about how much psychological damage they bestowed in the name of therapy.

Although this seems to be an isolated story, it is not at all unusual. In an article entitled "Dystonia: A Disorder Often Misdiagnosed as a Conversion Reaction," neurologists Ronald P. Lesser and Stanley Fahn state that, from the records of 84 patients who actually had dystonia, 37 had been originally diagnosed as mentally ill. They report, "These patients had received without benefit a variety of psychiatric therapies, including psychoanalysis for up to 2 years, psychoanalytic psychotherapy, behavioral therapy, hypnosis, and pharmacotherapy."[6]

A news story revealing the "Widespread and dangerous" medical doctor's misdiagnosis and referral to psychiatry states:

When 7-year-old Bailey Sheehan arrived at a hospital in Oregon partially paralyzed, a doctor said the girl was faking her symptoms to get her parents' attention because she was jealous of her new baby sister.

But that doctor was proved wrong when an MRI showed that the girl had acute flaccid myelitis or AFM, a polio-like disease that's struck hundreds of children since 2014. [7]

We are told by the experts how bad the misdiagnoses by medical doctors with their referrals to psychiatrists are:

Experts who study the art and science of diagnosis say the problem goes beyond this one rare disease. They say that in general, when presented with a puzzling disease, physicians too often leap to a diagnosis of a psychiatric problem.

"Mental disorders become the default position to deal with medical uncertainty," said Dr. Allen Frances, former chair of psychiatry at the Duke University School of Medicine. "It's widespread, and it's dangerous."

Dr. Mark Graber, president emeritus of the Society to Improve Diagnosis in Medicine, added, "It's a tendency that physicians have when they can't find a physical cause. It's bad. It's very bad.... Physicians have an obligation to do a thorough workup before turning to a psychological explanation," he said. [8]

The preceding cases are only examples of what can happen in this whole gray area of body/brain and mind. Many persons have been given psychotherapeutic treatment without success and were even hospitalized because they were suffering from some undetected physical disease or from inherited disorders like dystonia. The tragedy of it all continues even today.

There has been an unfortunate professional care division of brain/body and mind. What generally happens is that the medical doctor's main interest is with the brain/body, the psychiatrist's with both the brain/body and mind, and the psychotherapist's with the mind. The separation of mind from body is a naïve way of dealing with the total person. In fact, the total person also includes the spirit. Any system that regards one, such as the brain/body or the mind, without considering the other, and particularly the spiritual part of man, falls short of truly ministering to the whole person.

When God breathed into Adam, he became a living soul, whose spirit was alive and in communion with God Himself. Thus, human beings are more than flesh and blood and brain. They are living souls, endued with the nonphysical personhood of every individual who thinks, feels, decides, plans, wills, and loves. Nevertheless, the brain is an organ of the mind, and much needs to be learned about how a malfunction of the brain may affect the mental-emotional-behavioral condition of an individual.

Although mental problems are not always caused by spiritual problems, they can be and nonetheless should always be ministered to spiritually in addition to whatever else is done. In fact, every bodily ailment has spiritual implications and should likewise be ministered to on the spiritual level in addition to whatever other medical means are used.

Mental or Medical?

Psychiatrist Barbara Schildkrout sees the shortcomings of simply diagnosing according to the *DSM*. She has written two books to encourage her fellow practitioners to look beyond psychological symptoms. They are titled *Unmasking Psychological Symptoms: How Therapists Can Learn to Recognize the Psychological Presentation of Medical* Disorders[9] and *Masquerading Symptoms: Uncovering Physical Illnesses That Present as Psychological Problems.*[10] At the beginning of *Masquerading Symptoms* she quotes E. K. Koranyi:

> Non-specific behavioral and mood alterations often represent the very first and, occasionally for prolonged periods of time, the one single and exclusive sign of an undetected physical illness. Flagrantly and convincingly "psychological" in nature on presentation, such masked physical conditions frequently mislead the examiner and obliterate any further medical consideration, resulting in misdiagnosis and thus, inevitably, in treatment gone astray.[11]

Schildkrout then says:

> Many medical conditions can produce mental symptoms as their dominant clinical feature. This creates a diagnostic problem. How is one to know whether an underlying medical disease might be the cause of a patient's presenting psychological

symptoms? This question is a serious one for all mental healthcare practitioners, indeed for all clinicians.[12]

In her book, Schildkrout describes seventy different illnesses that may have psychological symptoms and may therefore elicit a misdiagnosis based on the categories of symptoms in the *DSM*, rather than a diagnosis associated with the actual illness. With many of the disease descriptions, she lists "Possible Presenting Mental Signs and Symptoms," and in another section she lists diseases "that may present with anxiety," a "depressed mood," "episodes of fear," and so on.[13]

Such misdiagnosis has been a long-standing concern with us. In our first book, *The Psychological Way/The Spiritual Way*, published in 1979, we have a brief section titled "Body/Mind: Misdiagnosis and Mistreatment," in which we describe cases in which people were misdiagnosed as having a mental problem when they were actually suffering from debilitating physical diseases. Schildkrout's book is a step in the right direction, and we hope many psychotherapists and medical doctors, particularly psychiatrists, internists, and family practice physicians, who are often the first to see a patient who is suffering mental distress, will read it.

In addition to known diseases, there may be excruciating mental-emotional symptoms for diseases not yet discovered. In fact there is a growing body of research indicating that mental, emotional, or behavioral symptoms may be caused by stealth germs in the body. Research is bringing to light the possibility that OCD (obsessive compulsive disorder) has its pathogenesis in certain viral organisms. The authors of "Viral Antibodies in Blood in Obsessive Compulsive Disorder" say:

> Obsessive Compulsive Disorder (OCD) is a relatively chronic disorder characterised by repeated thoughts, actions, impulses, ideas, images or actions, which are recognised as being irrational and are resisted. Although most of the earlier theorists regarded OCD to have a psychodynamic basis (Freud, 1909), recent work has focussed on its biological correlates (Jenike, 1984).[14]

Harvard Medical School posted a warning to parents of young children who suddenly develop strange behavior:

> With evidence mounting about the connection between infection and sudden-onset OCD, as the executive director of the International OCD Foundation, I helped coordinate two new public service announcements to help raise awareness that OCD and tic disorders can be triggered by infections in children. For many of these children, quick treatment with antibiotics can be the key to reversing OCD, tics, and other symptoms.[15]

> At the International OCD Foundation, we have heard heart-wrenching stories of well-adjusted children who develop sudden onset OCD. I have seen chilling before and after videos. One clip, with a time stamp of August 10, 2010, shows a typical, happy go lucky kid. The next clip, dated August 12, 2010, shows a screaming, terrified child and bewildered parents.[16]

This problem of misdiagnosis and maltreatment is not confined to medical doctors and psychotherapists. This serious problem has now ensconced itself in churches that refer their people to mental health systems and churches that do psychologically tainted biblical counseling. Unfortunately, it will be a long time, if ever, before pastors and other church leaders quit referring their people out to psychotherapists and psychologically influenced biblical counselors. If any referral is to be made at all, it should be to the person's own primary care doctor in case there is an underlying disease. Then, in addition to that referral, the body of Christ in the local fellowship should minister to the person, not with the assumption that the cause is spiritual, but rather to pray and bring biblical and practical help. When members of the body of Christ are suffering, others in the body need to encourage, comfort, pray, and respond through practical acts of mercy and help.

Conclusion

As scientific research reveals more and more about the mind-body connection within the context of living, we hope that more and more people will be helped. In the meantime, all of us need to take a humble look at ourselves and one another and not jump to conclusions about anyone's emotional problems. We are indeed "fearfully and wonderfully made" and we live in varying circumstances, all in the context of a universe created by God. We pray that as medical knowledge increases, there will be less misdiagnosis in the realm of the mind and emotions. We pray that Christians will seek God for solace in all these things, for He is the one who made us. He is the One who knows exactly what's going on in every individual and uses all for our spiritual good. We pray that referrals to psychotherapy (psychological talk therapy) will be replaced by mutual care among believers to help one another endure through trials and grow spiritually. Throughout every trial we are in our Father's care and He uses various trials, including illness, to conform us to the image of Christ (Rom. 8:28-29), until that day when we are given glorified bodies and see Jesus face to face.

Because of the vast spiritual needs of people who are enduring trials, medical doctors, psychiatrists, and psychotherapists would do well to refer their patients to the church for spiritual help and sustenance. As it is now, doctors and therapists refer patients to various religious practices in addition to the secular religion of psychotherapy. Patients are urged to participate in Yoga, Eastern forms of meditation, and guided imagery, but not Christianity.

Nearly 40 years ago one of the world's best-known psychiatrists, Dr. Thomas Szasz, recommended taking mental health care away from the professionals, such as M.D.'s and Ph.D.'s, and giving "this whole business back to the ministers and priests and rabbis."[17] This also would have meant taking it away from the Christians who are psychotherapists. If this had been done, both the mental and spiritual health of the nation could have dramatically improved—that is, if the church had not already fallen in love with psychotherapeutic theories and therapies. However, having lost much of its birthright through worldliness, much of the church would have been ill prepared, because the seminaries were already including too many of the ideas and techniques from the world of counseling psychology.

In a book titled *Crisis in Psychiatry and Religion*, O. Hobart Mowrer asks a penetrating question: "Has evangelical religion sold its birthright for a mess of psychological pottage?"[18] It's time for Christians to look objectively and prayerfully at the birthright and the mess of pottage.

4

The Medical Model
of Mental Illness

If you go to a medical doctor when you're physically sick, what's wrong with seeing a psychotherapist for mental-emotional-behavioral problems? That question is asked by those who confuse the use of medicine with the practice of psychotherapy, which is simply **conversation**. Individuals making such an error assume that the medical (physical) and the mental (nonphysical) can be thought of and talked about in the same manner and with the same terms. This error is one of using the medical model to justify the use of psychotherapy.

In the field of logic this is known as a *false analogy*. One logic text explains:

> An argument from analogy draws a conclusion about something on the basis of an analogy with or resemblance to some other thing. The assumption is that if two or more things are alike in some respects, they are alike in some other respect.[1]

In regard to a false analogy the text says:

To recognize the fallacy of false analogy, look for an argument that draws a conclusion about one thing, event, or practice on the basis of its analogy or resemblance to others. The fallacy occurs when the analogy or resemblance is not sufficient to warrant the conclusion.[2]

In the medical model physical symptoms are caused by some pathogenic agent. For example, a fever may be caused by viruses; remove the pathogenic agent and you remove the symptom. Or a person may have a broken leg; set the leg properly and the leg will heal. People have confidence in the medical model because it has worked well in the treatment of physical ailments. With the easy transfer of the model from medicine to psychotherapy, many people erroneously believe that mental problems can be thought of in the same say as physical problems.

Mental Illness

Applying the medical model to psychotherapy and its underlying psychologies came from the relationship between psychiatry and medicine. Since psychiatrists are medical doctors and since psychiatry is a medical specialty, many think that the medical model applies to psychiatry just as it does to medicine. Furthermore, psychiatry is draped with such medical trimmings as offices in medical clinics, hospitalization of patients, diagnostic services, prescription drugs, and therapeutic treatment. The very word *therapy* implies medical treatment. Further expansion of the use of the medical model to all of psychotherapy was easy after that.

The practice of medicine deals with the physical, biological aspects of a person; psychotherapy deals with the mental, emotional, and behavioral aspects. Whereas medical doctors attempt to heal the body, psychotherapists attempt to alleviate or cure mental, emotional, behavioral, and even spiritual suffering and to establish new patterns of thought and behavior. In spite of such dramatic differences, the medical model continues to be called upon to support the activities of the psychotherapist.

Additionally, the medical model supports the idea that a person with mental, emotional, or behavioral problems is ill in the sense that the **symptoms are the illness**, rather than the symptoms may indicate a physical disease. And with much sympathy we label people *mentally ill*, and we often categorize mental problems under the key term *mental illness*. Dr. Thomas Szasz adroitly explains it this way:

> If we now classify certain forms of personal conduct as illness, it is because most people believe that the best way to deal with them is by responding to them as if they were medical diseases.[3]

Psychotherapy deals with thoughts, emotions, and behavior, but not with the brain itself. Psychotherapy does not deal with the brain's biology, but with the mind's activity and the individual's social behavior. In medicine we understand what a diseased body is, but what is a parallel in psychotherapy? It is obvious that in psychotherapy *mental illness* does not mean *brain disease*. If brain disease were the case, the person would be a *medical* patient, not a *mental* patient.

Szasz very sharply refers to the "psychiatric impostor" who "supports a common, culturally shared desire to equate and confuse brain and mind, nerves and nervousness."[4]

Dr. Ronald Leifer, in his book *In the Name of Mental Health*, says:

> If we grant that in . . . medicine the term "disease" refers to the body, to modify it with the word "mental" is at worst a mixture of logical levels called a category error, and at best it is a radical redefinition of the word "disease." A category error is an error in the use of language that, in turn, produces errors in thinking. . . . Whatever the mind may be, it is not a thing like muscles, bones, and blood.[5]

Leifer discusses the arguments for the medical model and then the defects of such arguments. He concludes by saying:

> The principal advantages of this argument are therefore neither scientific nor intellectual. They are social. They prejudice the lay public to see psychiatric practices as more like medical treatment than like social control, socialization, education, and religious consolation. It bids them to presume that the psychiatrist, like other physicians, always serves the individual in his pursuit of life, health, and happiness.[6]

The use of the medical model in psychotherapy does not reveal truth; instead it merely disguises psychotherapy with a mask of jargon and ends up confusing everyone. Research psychiatrist E. Fuller Torrey says:

The medical model of human behavior, when carried to its logical conclusions, is both nonsensical and nonfunctional. It doesn't answer the questions which are asked of it, it doesn't provide good service, and it leads to a stream of absurdities worthy of a Roman circus.[7]

Using the medical model of human behavior and confusing *medical* with *mental* through a false analogy can lead to assuming that there is scientific support for ESP, past lives, UFOs, Eastern religions, and the occult. Transpersonal or religious psychologies are being supported through such false analogies and usage of the medical model.

The error of applying medical terminology to mental life causes erroneous thinking and responding. The very word *medical* carries with it the suggested treatment, for if we are dealing with an illness, medical treatment is implied. Therefore, whenever someone suggests that you should believe in psychotherapy because you believe in medicine, remember that *medical* and *mental* are **not** the same. **It is a false analogy and a false application of the medical model.**

Psychology grew out of philosophy. Each theory behind each therapy provides a philosophy of life and a theology of man—why we are the way we are and how we change. In fact, as we have shown elsewhere, psychotherapy is religion and not medicine.[8] After all, the word *psychology* comes from two words meaning the study of the soul. However, psychotherapists and their advocates misuse the medical model to support psychotherapy, even though they would not say their clients are mentally ill. They continue to make this false analogy to their own shame and to the detriment of others.

Instead of recognizing the fallacies of psychotherapy, many people have hailed it as a science and have trusted its conclusions, theories, and methods of diagnosis. Although it purports to be a science and attempts to align itself as such, it falls short of the objectivity and testability of science. Although it claims to dispense knowledge about the human condition, it has revealed few hard facts and has filled the vacuum with a collage of theories. Psychotherapy is not a coherent science in principle or in theory, diagnosis, or treatment. As a matter of fact, psychotherapy is a pseudoscience, as we have shown elsewhere.[9]

Mental Disorders

The Centers for Disease Control and Prevention say that during one year "about 25% of all US adults have a mental illness" and that "nearly 50% of US adults will develop at least one mental illness during their lifetime.[10] That means, according to this statistic, that about one in four adults suffers from a diagnosable mental disorder in a given year! *Mental illness*, *mental disease*, and *mental disorder* are the three terms most used to describe both medical and psychological conditions having to do with thinking, feeling, and behaving. These terms are too easily used to describe those who are suffering in the mental-emotional-behavioral realm with a nonorganic etiology. One encyclopedia gives *mental illness* as a synonym for *mental disorder*, and the National Alliance on Mental Illness says, "Mental illnesses are medical conditions."[11] We primarily use the terms *mental illness* and *mental disease*, but the term *mental disorder* is an equivalent to *mental illness* and *mental disease*. *Disorder* is a euphemistic way of referring to illnesses and diseases attributed to the mind and emotions by the mental health professions.

The question is whether the person has a literal disease or a metaphorical disease. As noted earlier, many medical diseases present themselves with mental, emotional, or behavioral symptoms and need to be referred to specialties other than psychiatry. Lumping the metaphorical with the literal puts everyone into a system that depends upon psychotherapy and/or psychotropic medications, rather than separating those suffering from disease or simply from circumstances of life and then correctly diagnosing those who are actually ill.

When Thomas R. Insel, MD, was the director of the National Institute of Mental Health he said the following:

> Mental disorders are among the most complex problems in medicine, with challenges at every level from neurons to neighborhoods. Yet, we know so little about mechanisms at each level. Too often, we have been guided more by religion than science. That is, so much of mental health care is based on faith and intuition, not science and evidence.[12]

Geneticist Dr. Steven McCarroll tells about his work in discovering the biological underpinnings of mental illnesses. He says:

> We are interested in (i) how the human genome varies from person to person, across and within human populations; and (ii) how genome varia-

tion affects molecular phenotypes in cells and tissues on its way to influencing disease risk in populations. We are particularly interested in how genome variation influences gene expression in neurons on its way to affecting brain phenotypes such as risk of bipolar disorder and schizophrenia.... Our goal is to use genetics to reveal the molecular pathophysiology of these disorders and generate new ideas for therapeutics.[13]

Indeed, there is a crying need to recognize the difference between issues and tissues and distinguish between metaphorical and literal forms of mental illness and mental disorder.

Mental Illness by Vote

To further confuse the mental illness metaphor issue, the Supreme Court has given additional support and credence to this metaphorical illness on the basis of vote. Previous to this psychotherapeutic era, drug addiction and alcoholism were considered to be social problems. In 1962 the Supreme Court ruled that drug addiction was a disease. Therefore a criminal sentence for having such a disease would violate the Eighth Amendment prohibition against cruel and unusual punishment. The court said:

> It is unlikely that any State at this moment in history would attempt to make it a criminal offense for a person to be mentally ill, or a leper, or to be afflicted with a venereal disease.... in the light of contemporary human knowledge, a law which made a criminal offense of such a disease would

doubtlessly be universally thought to be an infliction of cruel and unusual punishment.[14]

In Powell v. Texas, a 5 to 4 Supreme Court vote determined that alcoholism is a disease. **Two former social problems have now been transformed into illnesses by vote of the Supreme Court.** Harold Mulford, Director of Alcohol Studies at the University of Iowa, says:

> I think it's important to recognize that the alcohol disease concept is a propaganda and political achievement and not a scientific achievement. Science has not demonstrated that alcoholism is a disease by defining it, nor has science or technology demonstrated it to be a disease by coming up with an effective treatment or preventative.[15]

One professor says, "Labeling alcoholism a disease is like blaming the devil for our sins—it absolves us of responsibility for our actions."[16] R. E. Kendall says, "The disease concept of alcoholism [is] out of tune with the facts and a serious obstacle to rational solutions."[17]

Many are familiar with the fact that 58 percent of the psychiatrists voted in favor of deleting homosexuality from the list of mental illnesses. Apparently human behavior is vulnerable to votes of judicial and professional bodies in deciding what behavior is and what behavior is not a disease. Bruce Ennis and Thomas Litwack say of this psychiatric vote:

> If all that is needed to remove large numbers of individuals from the ranks of the mentally ill and grant them the status enjoyed by the rest of society is a vote by the American Psychiatric As-

sociation, then surely other diagnostic labels are also highly suspect.[18]

The measles, mumps, and chicken pox have not been subject to such a vote.

The buffoonery of the mental illness labeling game is further revealed when one considers the reason for the American Psychiatric Association (APA) decision about the status of homosexuality. Those who supported the removal of homosexuality from the list of illnesses did so on the grounds that the label *mental illness* should only apply to those who experience conflict about their condition. In other words, a homosexual who is disturbed about his condition is mentally ill; but, if he is comfortable with his orientation, he is not. The same is now true for pedophiliacs. In the light of such voting, a person's subjective evaluation about his own condition has now become a measure of whether or not he is sick, which reveals how fraudulent the mental illness labeling game is.

Such reasoning on the part of the APA extends the diagnostic authority to the person's own subjective evaluation of his condition, but this privilege of self diagnosis is now granted to many. For, if one is consistent, every condition considered to be a disease by the APA should be seen in the light of whether or not distress is present. If this subjective criteria were to be extended equally to all, such bizarre disorders as necrophilia (being sexually aroused by dead bodies) would only be considered a mental illness if the person felt disturbed about his condition. If the APA extended subjective criteria across the board there could be no involuntary confinement of anyone who did not consider himself mentally ill.

Sick Behavior?

Behavior that sickens is often called *sick*. In such a context the word is used as a metaphor to describe something that is disgusting or pathetic. Thus, the metaphor *sick* can be used as a label to criticize behavior that is bothersome. But, if such a label moves from a definition of *disgusting* or *pathetic* to one of *mental illness*, *mental disease*, or *mental disorder*, the original meaning of the term is altered or lost, and erroneous thinking follows when a metaphor becomes literal. The confusion of terms, such as *mental illness*, *sick behavior*, *mental disease*, and *mental disorder*, is illustrated in the following examples of people who exhibit irresponsible behavior but are not necessarily ill.

A man with a problem known as pedophilia wrote to a newspaper columnist. He complained that homosexuals can find satisfactory outlets for their desires, but not the pedophiliac. He wrote, "I am a professional man (certified public accountant), 40 years of age and the father of four young boys." Then he confessed, "I am attracted to little girls." The columnist replied, "When people are sick the only advice I can give is 'See a doctor,' and you are among the sickest."[19] That columnist quite regularly described certain behaviors as "sick." And, since she referred the person to a doctor, she obviously was not simply using a metaphor, but used the word in the literal, medical sense. However, she just said what the psychiatrists have proclaimed for years and what the public has come to believe: that behavior can be ill, diseased, or disordered.

Jim Jones started an experimental community in Guyana. As the result of a threatened investigation, Jones led members of his community into mass suicide. The final body count of hundreds included Jones himself. Before the awful incident in Guyana, all sorts of responsible and respectable persons praised Jim Jones. In fact, San Francisco medical doctor Carlton Goodlett had praised Jones as a person and complimented the Guyana experiment. Rosalyn Carter, wife of then President Jimmy Carter, dined with Jones in 1976, sent him a complimentary letter about a medical aid proposal of his, and later invited him to her husband's inauguration.

Numerous other dignitaries and celebrities admired both the man and what he was doing. However, the diagnosis by psychotherapists after the death drink orgy was predictably mental illness. And, the public predictably parroted that the man was sick. However, according to the many people closest to him, Jones was not sick before the incident. The only thing that changed about Jones before and after the Guyana incident (besides the fact that he died) was the opinion that people had about him.

Conclusion

The mental illness game has erected a safe scapegoat for human problems and, at the same time, has financially enriched psychotherapists, lawyers, and clients. Since such court settlements are usually paid for by large insurance companies, everybody wins except those who continue to pay escalating insurance premiums.

5

Disease. Diagnosis, and Prognosis

If a person literally has a disease, he needs proper diagnosis and treatment. On the other hand, if a person is experiencing problems of living, he needs to know what choices he can make to overcome the problems within the limitations of his own abilities and circumstances. If a Christian is experiencing problems of living, he can turn to God, the Bible, and other Christians for help. He has the Holy Spirit to help him choose God's way through the problems and exercise God's enablement for change.

Disease

Once mental-emotional-behavioral issues take on the disease or disorder concept, the so-called patient or client is treated by any number of psychological and medical therapies. Most of these can easily lead a person away from God and into self-effort or dependence on the counseling relationship. A Christian who is physically sick may need medical treatment, but one with problems of living needs biblical knowledge, wisdom, guidance, and godly loving support, not psychological treatment. Strangely enough, however, the psychological treatment has some of the same basic ingredients as exist in biblical ministry: rhetoric (talking) and religion.[1]

Dr. Thomas Szasz refers to the conversation of psychotherapy as "rhetoric." He says:

> In plain language, what do patient and psychotherapist actually do? They speak and listen to each other. What do they speak about? Narrowly put, the patient speaks about himself, and the therapist speaks about the patient. In a broader sense, however, both also speak about other persons and about various matters of concern to their lives. The point is that each tries to move the other to see or do things in a certain way. That is what qualifies their actions as fundamentally rhetorical. If the psychotherapist and his patient were not rhetoricians, they could not engage in the activity we now conventionally call *psychotherapy.*[2]

Lou Marinoff, a philosophy professor and president of the American Philosophical Practitioners Association wrote a book titled *Plato, Not Prozac!*[3] In it he proposes a therapeutic alternative to traditional psychotherapy called "philosophical counseling." One reviewer of Marinoff's book sums up his position as follows:

> Philosophical counseling (PC) is characterized by Marinoff as "therapy for the sane" (p. 11), and he objects strongly to what he sees as psychology and psychiatry's "disease-ifying" of mental health problems. He argues that emotional prob-

lems are not "mental illnesses" and that many modern-day difficulties are philosophical rather than psychological in nature. Therefore, philosophers, who presumably have acquired knowledge from studying what some of the greatest thinkers in history have said about a particular problem, are best equipped to assist clients in finding a philosophical theory to help navigate common difficulties arising in life.[4]

The disease concept for problems of living calls for professional treatment rather than personal responsibility. Such treatment falls under the category of medical or mental services, which fall into the category of health insurance coverage. Problems of living, therefore, must be transformed into illnesses, diseases, or disorders to be eligible for health insurance payments. In his book *The Powers of Psychiatry*, Dr. Jonas Robitscher points out how vague the concept of mental illness is and how unstable the definitions:

> The decision to see these people, and many others, as mentally ill or not so is entirely arbitrary, related not to the patient but to political and economic factors.[5]

In addition to the fraudulent confusion of mental illness, disease, or disorder with physical disease for purposes of health insurance payments, there is the use of the mental disease concept for disability payments. Psychiatrist Leonard Kurland describes what he calls a "colossal rip-off" scheme in which lawyers and psychiatrists "cooperate" for their own financial advantage, but to the disadvantage of the taxpayers. He says:

> Psychiatric disability in workers' compensation cases is a creation of lawyers, and is almost always a fraud—one that could not succeed without the participation of psychiatrists who sell their degrees as "medical adversaries."[6]

Kurland explains:

> The psychiatrist knows what to do: provide the attorney with a diagnosis of psychiatric disability and ascribe its origin to the patient's work situation.[7]

The term *mental illness* is confusing and deceptive and promotes cures for diseases which do not even exist. Robitscher concludes his chapter on defining *mental illness* by saying:

> The concept of mental disease remains vague, but the pragmatics of social functioning dictate that psychiatrists will continue to deal with people as if they are diseased whether or not the disease concept makes good sense ... since psychiatry has never been able to define mental disease, the medical basis for psychiatric authority must continue to be questioned, and the psychiatric decisions that rely on medical authority must always be scrutinized.[8]

The concept of sickness is a convenient psychological device to confuse people and to place great power and authority in the hands of the psychiatrists and psychotherapists. Once people are confused, it is easy to talk them into treatment and offer a cure. Therefore, the psychiatrist or psychologist must sustain the delusion of sickness in order to sell his supposed cures. As one writer puts it:

> Once we concede that people passively "catch" bad behavior from their environment in the same way they "catch" measles or bubonic plague, then it is up to the specialists to diagnose the disease and prescribe the cure.[9]

As society has trusted psychiatry and psychology more, its practitioners have upped the ante on the number of individuals in need of their help. Some years ago the national figure was ten percent and now some have irresponsibly estimated it to be as high as ninety-five percent.[10]

As we mentioned earlier, the *Diagnostic and Statistical Manual of Mental Disorders* published in 1952 had only 107 diagnoses of mental illness. Currently it includes a whopping near-300 mental disorders.[11] Dr. George Albee, past president of the American Psychological Association, says:

> Clearly the more human problems that we label mental illnesses, the more people that we can say suffer from them. And, a cynic might add, the more conditions therapists can treat and collect health-insurance payments for.[12]

Is this cynicism or realism?

Diagnosis

If the illness concept worked in practice, we might excuse its semantic inaccuracies. One measure of the usefulness of a medical concept of behavior is whether or not such a concept enables one to diagnose illness or wellness. Psychiatrist Walter Reich refers to diagnosis as "the central psychiatric act." He says that the psychiatrist's privilege to diagnose "gives him the power to control and to influence."[13] Since diagnosis is the illness concept put to the test, the question is: How good are psychotherapists at diagnosis?

In our book *The Psychological Way/The Spiritual Way* we quote research to show that psychological diagnosis is a disaster. It involves massive errors! Nonprofessionals are as good or better at it than professionals.[14] Psychiatrist Hugh Drummond admits, "Volumes of research have been done to demonstrate the absolute unreliability of psychiatric diagnosis."[15] In addition, studies have shown that the system cannot be relied upon to distinguish the sane from the insane in either civil or criminal matters.[16]

Drs. Herb Kutchins and Stuart Kirk, both university professors, say in their book *Making Us Crazy*:

> The illusion that psychiatrists are in agreement when making diagnoses creates the appearance of a united professional consensus. In fact, there is considerable professional confusion. Serious confusion about distinguishing mental disorders from nondisordered conditions and the inability of clinicians to use the manual reliably make the development and use of DSM vulnerable to a host of nonscientific pressures. If well-trained and well-intentioned therapists often fail to agree on specific diagnoses, how can the incompetent or purposely deceptive diagnostician be identified?[17]

In comparing diagnostic accuracy between professionals and lay persons, Dr. David Faust and Dr. Jay Ziskin say, "Studies show that professional clinicians do not in fact make more accurate clinical judgments than lay persons." As an example from research, they state, "Professional psychologists performed no better than office secretaries." Probably most damning to the professional is their statement: "Virtually every available study shows that amount of clinical training and experience are unrelated to judgmental accuracy."[18]

Albee tells how different therapists from different countries will disagree when presented with the same individuals. He refers to the usual psychiatric disagreements on mental fitness of the same defendants in court cases. The psychiatrists for the defense predictably have different opinions from those for the prosecution. And, it is consistently true that those considered affluent are generally given a more favorable diagnosis than those who are poor. Albee concludes, "Appendicitis, a brain tumor and chicken pox are the same everywhere, regardless of culture or class; mental conditions, it seems, are not."[19]

The system of diagnosis for mental illness in psychotherapy operates the opposite way from the system of guilt in jurisprudence. The court system protects the innocent party to such an extent that some who are guilty go free. This generosity in jurisprudence is reversed in psychotherapy. According to researcher David L. Rosenhan, who has done a classic study on psychological diagnosis and treatment, the therapist is more inclined to label a healthy person *sick* than a sick person *well*.[20] While jurisprudence bends over backwards to protect the innocent, psychotherapy is inclined to condemn the innocent for fear of making a mistake.

Szasz sadly states: "There is no behavior or person that a modern psychiatrist cannot plausibly diagnose as abnormal or ill.[21]

Christopher Lasch points out that:

> The psychiatric perversion of the concept of incompetence nullifies the rights of the accused.... He could prove his innocence, even in a rigged system of justice, more easily than he can establish his mental competence.[22]

In terms of justice, one is obviously better off being tried as a criminal than being diagnosed for mental illness. It is apparently more acceptable to have a criminal walking the streets than one with the dubious condition called mental illness.

Prognosis

Worse than the disaster of diagnosis is the problem of prognosis or prediction. After researching the ability of psychotherapists to predict a client's behavior, behavioral science professors Hillel Einhorn and Robin Hogarth conclude:

> It is apparent that neither the extent of professional training and experience nor the amount of information available to clinicians necessarily increases predictive accuracy."[23]

Psychotherapists have shown little validity in analysis of past behavior or in their predictions concerning future behavior of their clients. There is a paradox that "in spite of the great fallibility in professional judgment people seem to have unshakable confidence in it."[24] Robitscher says:

> Judges, juries, and the general public do not realize that many of the statements made by psychiatrists are based on common sense applied to data available to everyone. Because the opinion is expressed by an expert and because it is couched in an elaborate scientific vocabulary, its fallibility and its lack of special probative value are obscured.[25]

Forensic psychiatrist Ronald Schlensky reveals what many have suspected all along: "Psychiatrists are no better than other citizens in predicting a human being's conduct."[26]

Even the American Psychiatric Association has publicly admitted that psychiatrists cannot predict future dangerous behavior of their clients. In a court case involving murder committed by a person who had just seen a psychiatrist, the APA presented an amicus curiae brief. The brief stated that research studies indicate that psychiatrists cannot accurately predict the future potential dangerousness of a client.[27]

In a well-publicized Texas murder case, the American Psychiatric Association "told the Supreme Court that psychiatrists should be excluded from a part of the criminal process because their 'false claims to expertise' might mislead jurors."[28] Two psychotherapists urged a California Legislature Committee "to ban all psychiatric testimony in criminal trials." One attorney told the committee, "Psychiatrists will say, quite frankly, anything you want them to say."[29] These statements and others led

Idaho to eliminate mental illness as a defense in criminal cases, making it the first state to do so since the 1930's.[30]

Medical Disease and Metaphorical Disease

A paradox is evident when one compares physical diseases (medical) with metaphorical diseases (mental). In medicine when one has a real disease there exists the possibility for a real cure. In the area of the mind we are often dealing with nondiseases and noncures. In medicine where real diseases exist and real cures may be available, the patient has the freedom to refuse treatment. However, where so-called mental diseases are diagnosed and some type of therapy is offered, the person, once labeled and committed, has no freedom to refuse treatment. Szasz says:

> In the one area in which there is no real illness, and no real treatment, both the diagnosis and the treatment are compulsory. It's ironic, to say the least.[31]

Harold Mavritte, assistant director of programs for the Los Angeles County Department of Mental Health, says:

> When you come to rights, the mentally ill are the only ill people that can be detained against their will.... If a person is physically ill, you had better not treat him against his will unless it's a life or death matter and he's comatose.[32]

Psychiatrist Lee Coleman says:

> There's no other business where you can force someone to take your services—and then charge him for it. A medical doctor cannot force a patient

into a cast. But there are all sorts of legal proce-
dures to enable a psychiatrist to force treatment
on a patient.[33]

One professor said that unfortunately "most people
assume science will give black-and-white answers, when
some 90-plus percent of the time the best it can give us
is a 'maybe'" and that "scientists must help the courts
figure out what to do when 'maybe' is the best answer
science will ever be able to get."[34]

6

The Labeling Game

In addition to the vast errors of psychotherapeutic diagnosis and the inability to apply treatment with any certainty of cure, psychological diagnosis and treatment are fraught with other problems. Much of what is currently considered psychiatric illness is culture-bound.[1] Behavior which is not considered abnormal in one culture may be seen as normal in another culture. Even today, with the current interest in altered states of consciousness, behavior which would have previously been relegated to the mental illness category is now seen as something to be desired. For instance, "out-of-the-body" or certain types of hallucinatory experiences would have served as symptoms of mental illness just a few years ago. What was considered a symptom in the past may be considered a solution today. Also, what may be considered "well" behavior today may be considered mental illness tomorrow.

Culture Bound

Psychiatrist E. Fuller Torrey declares that "cures" are also both culture-bound and class-bound.[2] Studies have shown that those of the lower socio-economic class are given the label *mentally ill* much more readily than those of the middle and upper classes.

Dr. Hugh Drummond reports:

> The more the doctor likes the patient, which by and large means the closer they are in social class, the more likely he is to diagnose the patient as neurotic rather than psychotic. Poor people, blacks and Hispanics are quickly labeled "psychotic" or "character-disordered" for the *same behavior* that earns white, middle-class patients the label "neurotic" (i.e., relatively healthy).[3] (Italics in original.)

One book reports how "the mental health movement is unwittingly propagating a middle-class ethic under the guise of science."[4]

The enthusiastic reception of the American Psychiatric Association's *Diagnostic and Statistical Manual of Mental Disorders*, with its standardized descriptions of typical American forms of mental suffering has homogenized mental anguish all over the world. This worldwide spread of American concepts of mental illness is called by some, "American psychiatric imperialism." This very accusation is documented with specific worldwide examples in a book that reveals how this has occurred. The jacket cover says:

> In *Crazy Like Us*, Ethan Watters reveals that the most devastating consequence of the spread of American culture has not been our golden arches or our bomb craters but our bulldozing of the human psyche itself: We are in the process of homogenizing the way the world goes mad....

We categorize disorders, thereby defining mental illness and health, and then parade these seemingly scientific certainties in front of the world. The blowback from these efforts is just now coming to light: It turns out that we have not only been changing the way the world talks about and treats mental illness—we have been changing the mental illnesses themselves.

For millennia, local beliefs in different cultures have shaped the experience of mental illness into endless varieties. *Crazy Like Us* documents how American interventions have discounted and worked to change those indigenous beliefs, often at a dizzying rate.[5]

In the former USSR the psychiatric label was used as an insidious tool of the government to punish and incarcerate political dissidents. *Time* quotes exiled writer Vladimir Bukovsky at the time as saying:

It is not easy for the ordinary person to get admitted for treatment in a psychiatric hospital. For a political case, though, it is very easy. They are taken to a hospital without making any request.[6]

In fact he says that the accused is not allowed to attend his own trial because he is mentally ill. Thus, the label *mental illness* is used instead of a fair trial and the length of sentence can be extended as long as the person is labeled *mentally ill*.

Similar abuses are evidenced in our society; this shows to what extent a contrived disease and so-called cure can be manipulated. Professor Christopher Lasch says:

> Today the state controls not merely the individ-
> ual's body but as much of his spirit as it can pre-
> empt; not merely his outer but his inner life as
> well; not merely the public realm but the darkest
> corners of private life formerly inaccessible to
> political domination.[7]

With the rise of psychiatry and psychotherapy there has
been a reduction of personal freedom through the use of
the label *mental illness*.

Besides the problems of mental illness as a concept,
of diagnosis as a practice, and of the political-social-
economic implications, there are further problems which
come from hanging a diagnostic label on an individual.
Such labeling can promote a self-fulfilling prophecy.
That is, if someone is treated in a particular manner, he
may begin to act accordingly. Also, once a label is placed
on a person, other people tend to react to that person according to the label. If told that someone is mentally ill,
people are apt to view what he says or does in terms of
his so-called illness.

Once the label has been attached, professionals tend
to use every statement and action as a kind of confir-
mation of that label. Psychiatrist Walter Reich refers to
the self-confirmation involved in the process of diagnosis and says that "anything a diagnosed patient says or
does, even in his own defense, can be cited as a symptom
of his illness—even if the diagnosis itself is incorrect."[8]
Studies show a common tendency to view behavior according to the presence or absence of a label.[9]

DSM and Devious Diagnoses

Four medical doctors from the University of California, San Diego, used the *DSM* in their attempt to diagnose a person from the past, whom they had never met. In the *Archives of General Psychiatry* Eric Lewin Altschuler et al. consider whether Samson from the Bible (Judges 13-16) had Antisocial Personality Disorder (ASPD). They say, "The *DSM*-IV requires that 3 of the criteria be met for the diagnosis of ASPD. Samson meets 6." They list the 6 with the verses from Judges as proof:

> "(1) Failure to conform to social norms with respect to lawful behavior" (ref. Judges 15:6; 16:1).

> "(2) Deceitfulness, as indicated by repeated lying" (ref. Judges14:9).

> "(3) Impulsivity" (ref. Judges 15:5).

> "(4) Irritability and aggressiveness" (ref. his various physical fights).

> "(5) Reckless disregard for safety of self or others" (ref. Judges 15:15; 16:17).

> "(6) Lack of remorse" (ref. Judges 15:16).

These medical doctors contend that the ASPD started when Samson was quite young. However, they assure their readers that "Samson shows no evidence of schizophrenia" and that "Some of his behaviors . . . seem to have been done during a nonmanic state."[10]

This is only one of a number of paradoxes in psychiatry. On the one hand, the psychiatric profession wants to be regarded as scientific in the classification of human behavior. On the other hand, they reveal the unscientific nature of their means of classification and diagnosis of disease by their labeling contradictions. They saddle Samson with a diagnostic label without so much as a diagnostic interview (as subjective as that is)..

Altschuler and his colleagues labeled Samson ASPD according to an unreliable *DSM* system. In contrast, the Bible lists Samson as a man of faith (Hebrews 11:32). True believers will take the Word of God over the *DSM* worldly wisdom, about which we are warned in Scripture.

Altschuler has also pilloried the prophet Ezekiel with a nonsensical neurological nosology (systematic classification of disease). According to an article in *The New Scientist*, Altschuler "says that records in the Bible reveal that Ezekiel, who lived about 2600 years ago, showed extreme classic symptoms of temporal lobe epilepsy." The article reveals Altschuler's findings as follows:

> Neurologically Ezekiel displayed some obvious signs of epilepsy, such as frequent fainting spells and episodes of not being able to speak.
>
> The Biblical figure, who chronicled the fall of Jerusalem in 586 BC, exhibited other peculiarities associated with the disease. For instance, he wrote compulsively, a trait known as hypergraphia. Altschuler points out that the Book of Ezekiel is the fourth longest in the Bible—only slightly shorter than Genesis. "It's impenetrable," he says. "He goes on and on."

Ezekiel was also extremely religious, another characteristic associated with this form of epilepsy. While many Biblical figures are pious, none was as aggressively religious as Ezekiel, says Altschuler. Other signs of epilepsy can include aggression, delusions and pedantic speech—and the man had them all.[11]

Altschuler *et al* have already shown disrespect for Samson (a Judge of Israel and listed among the examples of faith in Hebrews 11) by considering him a psychiatric case and slamming him with the *DSM* label ASPD. Then Altschuler adds insult to injury against the Bible by explaining away the prophet Ezekiel's divine calling by describing his work as "extreme classic symptoms of temporal lobe epilepsy."

Altschuler claims to have seen something significant in Ezekiel, but his lack of faith in the Bible and in its divine inspiration blinds him to the truth, and so he must turn to nonsensical neurological myths to understand the complexity of Ezekiel. Altschuler provides one more example of the contrast between the wisdom of men and the Word of God and one more example of the foolishness of the worldly-wise.

Now we will guess at a diagnosis for Altschuler et al., based upon a perfect, valid, and reliable "system" of diagnosis called the Bible. The Bible describes the fool: "The fool hath said in his heart, there is no God" (Psalms 14:1). Any fool, believing there is no God and that the Bible is not the very Word of God, can make any foolish and faulty diagnosis according to any worldly system.

Disease Mongering

Also, be aware of what is called "disease mongering" (DM). DM occurs in the following way: A "disease" is discovered and a profile is created. Once that profile is created and the disease named, patients will see themselves in the profile and therapists will see the patient through that profile and ipso facto a diagnosis is made and a prescription written. Example: Oppositional Defiant Disorder (ODD) is a label applied to children and adolescents. The symptoms are such that most children have acted in most of the behaviors on the list. The parent and the doctor will then see the child through the symptoms and oftentimes a prescription is written and counseling arranged.

Drummond gives an example to reveal how easy it is to become entangled in the whole process of viewing a person as abnormal. He refers to a study which used verbatim transcripts of individuals who "led normal lives and had average scores on psychological tests." A group of psychiatrists were told that the individuals were patients and were asked for a diagnosis. Drummond reports, "Forty percent of the psychiatrists chose 'acute paranoid schizophrenia' to describe these examples of normal verbal behavior." He goes on to say," One result of the study was particularly upsetting: the more experienced the psychiatrist, the more likely he or she was to choose a more pathological diagnosis." Drummond states, "While schizophrenia is considered a 'medical diagnosis' like pneumococcal pneumonia or appendicitis, it actually functions as a degradation ritual imposed upon those who have broken some rules of propriety."[12]

The label *mental illness* may be used to excuse and/ or condemn persons with some form of unacceptable behavior. Quite often elderly adults, who may be very strong-willed and who might not be willing to act the way relatives and neighbors want them to act, come under such diagnostic labels. Rather than helping them cope with life, labeling and treating such persons often make them confused and unable to cope as well as before such "help" is imposed.

Reich describes such a case of a woman whose main problem was that she was "negative and disagreeable" in that she was more dogmatic about her opinions and made remarks that embarrassed family members. The diagnosis by the chief psychiatrist upon hospital admission was "organic brain syndrome." However, a young resident could see no reason for that label. He was over-ruled and no matter how hard the woman denied having the difficulties ascribed to her, she continued to be treated as mentally ill. Incarcerated in a ward without anyone to pay real attention to what she was saying, she was continually misunderstood. Reich says, "The more she denied illness, the more powerfully the diagnosis was maintained."[13]

Then, when the woman decided to cooperate with the hospital procedure, her change of behavior went unnoticed. Finally she became discouraged and angry and was thus further diagnosed as having a "catastrophic reaction." The "solution" was to put her on a heavy tranquilizer, which calmed her down and further "proved" the original diagnosis. No one, except the young resident, even thought to doubt the original diagnosis, and all subsequent behavior was seen and treated in the light of "organic brain syndrome."[14] Unfortunately stories like this abound, much to the chagrin of the professionals and much to the distress, despair, and devaluation of the victims.

Conclusion

The very term *mental illness* or *mental disorder* has become a blight to society. The mystique surrounding it has frightened away people who could be of great help to those suffering from problems of living. Many people who want to help individuals with problems of living feel unqualified to help a person labeled *mentally ill* or *mentally disordered*. The confusion inherent within this strange juxtaposition of terms has led to errors which have often been more harmful than helpful to those thus labeled. Nevertheless, the profession continues to proliferate the false concept of mental illness, to align it with medicine, and consign it to science—and the public and church follow.

7

Mental Illness and Irresponsibility

The terms *mental illness*, *mental disease*, and *mental disorder* are popular catch-alls for all kinds of problems of living, many of which have little or nothing to do with illness. As soon as a person's behavior is labeled *illness*, *disease*, or *disorder*, treatment by psychotherapy or biblical counseling becomes the so-called solution. If, on the other hand, we consider a person to be responsible for his behavior, we should deal with him in the areas of education, faith, and choice. If we label him *mentally ill* (*diseased* or *disordered*) we rob him of the human dignity of personal responsibility and the divine relationship by which problems may be met.

To begin with, **the word *mental* means "mind" and the mind is not the same as the brain.** Also, the mind is really more than just a function or activity of the brain. Brain researcher Dr. Barbara Brown insists that the mind goes beyond the brain. She says:

> The scientific consensus that mind is only mechanical brain is dead wrong ... the research data

of the sciences themselves point much more strongly toward the existence of a *mind-more-than-brain* than they do toward mere mechanical brain action.[1]

Dr. Arthur Custance, in his book *The Mysterious Matter of Mind,* presents,

> ...the experimental findings of recent research which have led some of the most renowned scientists in the field to conclude that *mind is more than matter* and more than a mere by-product of the brain.[2]

The Bible raises the level of human dignity far above that of a physical organism. Not only has God created humans with minds which can think, reason, choose, and direct action; He has also created man in His own image with a spiritual dimension.

> So God created man in his own image, in the image of God created he him; male and female created he them. (Genesis 1:27.)

God created the human mind to know Him and to choose to love, trust, and obey Him. In the very creative act, God planned for mankind to rule His earthly creation and to serve as His representatives on earth (Genesis 1:26-28). Because the mind goes beyond the physical realm, it goes beyond the reaches of science and cannot be medically sick.

Psychological counseling does not even deal with the brain itself. Instead, it deals with aspects of thinking, feeling, and behaving. Therefore, psychotherapists are not in the business of healing illnesses, diseases, or disorders, but rather of teaching new ways of thinking, feeling, and behaving. They are actually teachers, including those who are medical doctors who are psychiatrists practicing psychotherapy. Harvard psychiatrist Shervert Frazier, former chairman of the American Psychiatric Association Joint Commission on Public Affairs, says, "Psychotherapy is a form of education."[3] Nevertheless, many psychotherapists perpetuate the concept of mental illness, disease, or disorder, and people follow the fallacy.

Many have wrongfully used the term *mental* with the terms *illness, disease,* and *disorder* to describe a whole host of problems of thinking, feeling, and behaving which should be labeled as "problems of thinking, feeling, and behaving." Though the term *mental illness* (*disease, disorder*) is usually a misnomer and a mismatch of words, it has become firmly ingrained in the public vocabulary and is glibly pronounced on all sorts of occasions by both lay and professional persons. In his book *The Powers of Psychiatry*, Jonas Robitscher, M.D., J.D., says:

> Our culture is permeated with psychiatric thought. Psychiatry, which had its beginnings in the care of the sick, has expanded its net to include everyone, and it exercises its authority over this total population by methods that range from enforced therapy and coerced control to the advancement of ideas and the promulgation of values.[4]

The mistake is reinforced continually until one sees mental illnesses, diseases, or disorders wherever one turns and turns whatever one sees into mental illness, disease, or disorder.

The kinds of problems of living normally talked about with a psychotherapist, unless medically driven, are spiritual problems calling for biblical ministry, not psychological problems needing psychological solutions. The church has been duped into believing that problems of living are problems that require psychological therapy, rather than problems of the soul that call for biblical ministry. This erroneous conclusion was reached through the use of the term *mental* with the terms *illness, disease, and disorder*, which are metaphors that are molded to fit everything from brain diseases to problems of living having to do with feeling, thinking, and acting. This chameleon-like concept is the crux of the confusion that causes committed Christians to be conned into catastrophic conclusions about counseling. Problems of living absent biological underpinnings are not mental illnesses, diseases, or disorders!

In addition to the inherent weaknesses and problems associated with the concepts of mental illness, mental disease, and mental disorder, such concepts often violate certain biblical principles, particularly those of personal responsibility. The idea of illness, disease, or disorder in the mental realm conveys the notion that those afflicted are not responsible for their behavior. If individuals with mental-emotional-behavioral problems are "sick," it often follows that they are no longer considered responsible for their behavior. And, if they are not responsible for their behavior, who is? Where does one draw the line?

The disease metaphor easily slips into other areas of life and takes on such literal meaning that personal responsibility for behavior is overshadowed. In his book *The Seven Deadly Sins Today*, Henry Fairlie suggests that therapies have exonerated man from responsibility. He says:

> A hundred little -ologies spawn a thousand little therapies, for ourselves and our societies, and what we think we have discovered for the first time we place before all the knowledge of the past, thus further releasing ourselves to do simply what we will.[5]

In terms of will, it is obvious that those who are experiencing only problems of living, not complicated by biological involvement, have a much greater degree of choice in thought and action than those who have organic brain disease. God holds each person responsible to the extent that choice exists for him. It is naïve to state that all men have the same level of choice and are therefore equally responsible. Nevertheless, as we say in Chapter 1: In this perilous, peculiar, and puzzling area of not truly knowing whether or not a mental-emotional-behavioral issue or disorder is biological or spiritual, one can nevertheless assume that **people are responsible for their behavior and can benefit from biblical ministry**.

Insanity Defense

Psychiatrist E. Fuller Torrey is one of the leading psychiatric researchers in America and has extensively studied schizophrenia and bipolar behavior. He is thoroughly knowledgeable about psychiatric testimony and the insanity defense. He says, "The ultimate in the concept of nonresponsibility for mental 'patients' is the insanity defense."[6] Typically in court cases where the insanity defense is claimed for the defendant, psychiatrists are used for and against the defense. Torrey comments on this practice by saying: "Although the psychiatrist takes the witness stand as a 'scientist,' he has nothing to offer the court on this matter except the same subjective evaluation of the criminal as any other man."[7] Torrey says: "Psychiatrists really have no more right to decide who is guilty and not guilty than does the Good Humor man."[8] Torrey further states:

> Seymour Halleck, a psychiatrist who has studied the issue extensively, sounds a similar note: "Medical involvement in issues of criminal responsibility is without a scientific basis, is socially impractical, and has probably done harm both to society and to the psychiatric profession."[9]

In the no-man's-land between a high degree of responsibility (sanity) and no responsibility (insanity), the California court system permits a defense plea called "diminished capacity." This was the plea of Dan White after he murdered both San Francisco Mayor George Moscone and San Francisco Supervisor Harvey Milk. The court agreed that White could not be tried for first-degree murder because of diminished capacity. Instead, he received a light sentence on manslaughter charges, was released from prison, and later committed suicide. Since then the door has been wide open for similar pleas, and criminals who know exactly what they are doing will escape whatever just punishment they deserve through the loophole of diminished capacity. This plea is the understandable result of the misnomer of *mental illness* and the influence of secular humanism. The combination of these two mistakes results in a pseudosickness which is supposedly caused by society rather than self, since man is seen as good but corrupted by biology and/or circumstances.

A twenty-nine-year-old businesswoman was a passenger on a San Francisco cable car when it rolled backwards and crashed. She sued the Municipal Railway for $500,000, claiming that the accident had resulted in the mental disease "nymphomania." During her trial she told of having over one hundred lovers since the accident and confessed that at one point she had engaged in sexual intercourse fifty times in five days. The psychiatric explanation suggested that the pole she was thrown against in the accident represented her stern Lutheran father and that this somehow led to severe "psychic trauma."[10]

Ethan Anthony Couch killed four people while driving under the influence with a blood alcohol content of 0.24, which is three times the legal limit. At the same time he was tested positive for marijuana and valium. "He was intoxicated, driving on a restricted license and speeding in a residential area when he lost control, colliding with a group of people assisting another driver with a disabled SUV. Four people were killed in the collision and a total of nine people were injured. Two passengers in Couch's truck suffered serious bodily injury, one with complete paralysis...." The judge "sentenced Couch to ten years of probation and subsequently ordered him to therapy at a long-term in-patient facility after his attorneys argued that the teen had 'affluenza' and needed rehabilitation instead of prison." The psychologist testified that Couch was a "product of affluenza," because he learned growing up that "wealth buys privilege."[11]

With respect to the insanity plea, Dr. Thomas Szasz says it succinctly in the following:

What is wrong with the insanity plea is that it creates an impression that it is not the person but the insanity that does something.[12]

One medical doctor, for example, refers to the "psychosis which apparently led John Hinckley, Jr., to his despicable attack on our [former] president."[13]

Rousas Rushdoony says:

> If my criminal behavior is not a moral fault in me but a social disease for which a disorderly society is to blame, I am then a victim, not an offender.

He concludes:

> Men find it easier to claim a sickness for which society is held responsible, than to affirm a moral model, which requires them to confess, "I acknowledge my transgressions: and my sin is ever before me. Against thee, thee only, have I sinned, and done this evil in thy sight" (Psalms 51:3-4).[14]

Elsewhere Rushdoony says, "The cult of victimization is perhaps the most popular religion of our time."[15]

Psychotherapy deals with individuals almost entirely as victims, rarely as sinners. Everyone is a victim of one sort or another, past or present. It is therefore easy to identify and to magnify the victim role, and soon it becomes the sole orientation of the individual. Rushdoony says:

> A great deal of our bigotry comes from a concentration on the wrongs we have suffered rather than on the wrongs we inflict on other people. No lying is involved, only an emphasis on one aspect of our lives.

Rushdoony reminds us, "There is not a group in society which has not suffered some indignities and also inflicted indignities on others." He asks, "Can you convince any group of their sins?" and concludes, "They have to major in the sins of others."[16] Treating a person as a victim will only amplify the problem.

In his book *A Nation of Victims: The Decay of the American Character*, Charles Sykes says:

> Blaming one's ills on oppression, on society, on psychological maladjustment, on racism, or on sexism is tempting because those complaints provide clarity and certitude — and perhaps even identity as part of a *faux* community of victims. Such self-diagnoses are perhaps inevitable for a society that has grown unwilling to judge itself in terms of moral or personal responsibility.[17]

Sykes does not deny that there are real victims in some of these areas. However, he is concerned about the result of making everyone a victim. He says;

> The challenge of the politics of victimization is to those who *do* care about genuine victims and who recognize that victimism reaps its advantage at the direct expense of those most deserving of compassion and support. *If everyone is a victim, then no one is.*[18] (Italics in original.)

Human will and responsibility go hand in hand. If a person makes choices, then he is accountable for his behavior. Individuals have different degrees of freedom of choice because of biological limitations, environmental background, habits established through past choices, and the other effects of the Fall. However, God holds each person responsible for the degree of choice he possesses. A person is not responsible for all that happens to him, but he is responsible for his reactions. The Bible makes it clear that people do make choices and are held accountable for their behavior.

The principle of personal responsibility and accountability is a critical biblical doctrine. According to Scripture, man chooses his thoughts, attitudes, and actions. People choose to love and to hate, to forgive and to accept forgiveness, to act responsibly or irresponsibly, and to think biblically or unbiblically. God created humankind with a will—the capacity to choose. He has also endowed humankind with a conscience to assist the will. He has commanded and exhorted humankind regarding love and forgiveness, thoughts and actions. Moreover, He has given new life to believers to enable them to do what is right according to the Bible.

Torrey has written a chapter on people as human beings in his book *The Death of Psychiatry*. We asked and received his permission to use the following:

> The uniqueness of human beings lies in our self-consciousness which allows us to be responsible for our actions. Depriving human beings of this responsibility is the ultimate insult, for it consigns us to less-than-human status.
>
> This is exactly what the medical model of human behavior does. It sees human behavior as determined by such things as biochemical predispositions and the experiences of childhood. Human beings in this view become machines determined by forces beyond their control and it is these

forces which determine what the person will do. The human, rather than being free, becomes a prisoner of the id and chemicals of the brain. Freud represented this point of view *par excellence* when he described man's behavior as the product of intrapsychic forces, forces which were exerted through a plumber's nightmare of cerebral pipes, valves, gauges, and pressure outlets.

Such a view of human beings ignores our uniqueness—the peculiar arrangement of our brain cells which allow us to contemplate ourselves and our actions. We can assess the effects of past actions and plan the probabilities of future actions. As such, we have a freedom of behavior that is not enjoyed by lower animals.

The medical model deprives us of this freedom of behavior. By viewing us as a machine and our behavior as determined by forces beyond our control, proponents of the medical model have been able to arrive at the idea of nonresponsibility. People who are mentally "ill" are those whose forces have gotten out of control. As such they cannot be held responsible. This leads logically to things like declaring people unfit to stand trial, involuntary confinement, and the insanity defense, a panoply of prejudice and partiality that besmirches our judicial scene.

When the medical model of human behavior is discarded the concept of nonresponsibility is discarded as well. People become fully responsible for their actions. And since there is no group of people called the mentally "ill," there is no group who can be called not responsible and thereby deprived of their uniqueness as human beings. **The only exceptions to this are the small group of people who have actual brain disease. These people, in some cases, may not be responsible for their behavior.**[19] (Bold added.)

Torrey gives examples of this "small group of people who have actual brain disease" and in some cases "may not be responsible for their behavior": "the man with brain syphilis (who thought his wife was trying to poison him) and the woman with a brain tumor (who had propositioned two men on the street)."[20]

However, Torey calls for caution:

And until we have more precise indicators, it is best that we err on the side of labeling too few, rather than too many, as brain diseased. In other words, a person should be assumed *not* to have a brain disease until proven otherwise on the basis of probability. This is exactly the opposite of what we do now as we blithely label everyone who behaves a little oddly as "schizophrenic." Human dignity rather demands that people be assumed to be in control of their behavior and not brain diseased unless there is strong evidence to the contrary.[21] (Italics in original.)

Torrey additionally says:

The underlying principle which I am utilizing to judge human behavior is the assumption that a person is responsible until it is proven (on the basis of probability at least) that he is not. Human dignity demands that much as a minimum…. If we have to err, it is better that we err on the side of human dignity and call too few, rather than too many, people "sick."

One of the most important consequences of accepting these people as responsible is that they will be encouraged to accept that responsibility themselves.[22]

The mental-illness way generally misses man's ability to choose and his responsibility to do so because of the concept of the medical model of mental illness. Calling someone a pedophiliac, egomaniac, nymphomaniac, alcoholic, or drug addict with the added label "mentally ill" denies willful choice. It removes moral responsibility and thus reduces the possibility for improvement. Increasing a person's awareness that he can and does choose and that he is responsible for his thoughts and behavior increases his possibility for change. Robitscher says that people are labeled:

…as mentally ill for social reasons that have nothing to do with concepts of health and disease. We label people mentally ill to give them the benefit of a psychiatric excuse: so a student can continue in college even though he has not taken his examinations, or so a woman will not be sent to prison even though she has murdered her baby. Whether these people are mentally ill or not does not seem very important; the label of mental illness is needed to justify what we feel needs to be done.[23]

Labeling a person's behavior as "sick" and giving him the accompanying psychological excuse reduces the possibilities for improvement. Treating a person's behavior as an illness only convinces him that he cannot choose to change on his own. The responsibility for behavior and change is thus transferred from the person to the therapist. Therapy then replaces responsibility. Psychiatrist Peter Breggin, founder of the Center for the Study of Psychiatry, says:

> It becomes increasingly difficult to help patients take responsibility for their lives because psychiatry itself is telling them that they aren't responsible.[24]

Unless a person is held responsible for his behavior, he will tend not to be responsible. Teaching an individual that he can choose and is responsible for his behavior will set the stage for needed change. Once a person accepts the fact that he does have a choice and that he is accountable, improvement follows. Larry Thomas, a professor of journalism, says:

> We have fabricated physiological, psychological, and sociological causes for the woes that beset mankind. We have created a guiltless society in which people are no longer responsible for their actions. We have ignored sin and found either a medical, emotional or social phenomenon to blame for our problems.[25]

Conclusion

Only a very small number of individuals with symptoms of mental illness are literally brain diseased and therefore "may not be responsible for their behavior." However, this number is likely amazingly small compared to the nearly 300 *DSM* mental disorders. Therefore, the insanity plea should be carefully examined case by case with the understanding that very few are entitled to such coverage. Eventually scientific explanations into the brain/mind and body will reveal more. In the meantime, **all those with mental-emotional-behavioral disorders can be and should be ministered to biblically**, as we have done for years. Those with medically established disease should have the option to be in any necessary medical treatment.

8

Organically Generated Difficulties?

The first great mistake of many counselors is the adoption of and reliance on the psychological counseling format of problem-centeredness, which results in sinful conversations. The second great error of biblical counselors and many Christians is based on the lack of objective biological markers for nearly all of the almost 300 *DSM* designations of mental disorders. Many Christians come to the worst conclusion by assuming that if there are no objective biological markers, there is no medical reason for mental-emotional-behavioral symptoms. Period! Others believe that, if a complete medical exam reveals no medical causes, there is therefore no medical illness to account for the symptoms. These Christians erroneously conclude that no objective biological markers equals no mental illness. Therefore, they further conclude that the mental-emotional-behavioral symptoms are due to a spiritual problem in need of a biblical solution with the unspoken message that if individuals do not improve, it is spiritually their fault.

As we indicate in Chapter 1: In **most cases** of personal ministry, it is both not possible and not necessary to know for sure whether or not such disorders or challenges are the result of an objective biological illness. However, when no objective biological markers exist, one should not assume that a particular mental-emotional-behavioral issue is or is not the result of a spiritual problem. In fact, it is not always necessary to know whether or not a bodily problem is the cause of a trial, tribulation, or suffering. That is because biblical care has to do with ministering the Word of God in mercy, compassion, and patience, with the realization that one cannot truly know whether the body, soul, and/or spirit are driving a particular behavior or mental disorder. Even if there is knowledge of an accompanying disease that may cause or add to the suffering, much humility is required, because the one who ministers will generally not know the exact reasons behind a person's particular feelings or behavior. To assume that one Christian can analyze another person's soul to determine motivation or reasons behind that person's behavior is biblically wrong and can lead to spiritual misdiagnosis.

The one who ministers need not assume that the one in need has a spiritual problem needing a biblical solution, but one should always minister biblically, trusting the Holy Spirit to work out the unknowables. In humility and dependence on the Holy Spirit, believers are called to minister to those in need, according to God's Word in the fellowship of the saints, in spite of any mental-emotional-behavioral labels. One should never assume that the one receiving ministry has a spiritual problem unless it is transparent that their behavior violates Scripture.

Neither should one attempt to diagnose another person's specific spiritual condition by trying to analyze another person's soul. Absent external evidence, one should not conclude that a person's trial, tribulation, or suffering is due to one of the seven deadly sins or some inner "idol of the heart." Such attempts lead to guesswork based on counseling conversations filled with sinful speaking that feeds the old nature (see Chapter 9). **Such attempts to see and reveal a person's inner soul usurp the prerogative of the Holy Spirit.** One who ministers should always minister spiritually according to the Bible with teaching and encouragement to walk according to the Spirit rather than the flesh (old carnal nature).

As we say in Chapter 1 and elsewhere, we recommend that Christians who minister to others begin with the understanding that individuals, regardless of their mental-emotional-behavioral symptoms or designations, can be ministered to, **as long as a rational conversation can take place and that the content of the conversation is undergirded by love and biblically-based**. We again repeat from Chapter 1: In this perilous, peculiar, and puzzling area of not truly knowing whether or not a mental-emotional-behavioral issue is biological or spiritual, one can nevertheless assume that **people are responsible for their behavior and can benefit from biblical ministry**.

Counseling the Hard Cases (*CTHC*), coauthored by seminary professors Stuart Scott and Heath Lambert, is a book dedicated to the mistaken idea that, if there are no objective biological markers, there is no medical illness. In this chapter we discredit that idea. In an attempt to prove that they can do as well or better than their psychological counterparts, popular leaders of the biblical counseling movement describe ten counseling cases.[1]

In Chapter 3 of our critique of *CTHC*, titled "'Organically Generated Difficulties'?" we expose serious errors of these ten biblical counselors, which begin with their mistaken notion that no objective biological markers means no medical illness. They proceed as if one can always know if there is a medical illness and therefore know whether one surely has a spiritual root to a problem. These erroneous assumptions, along with the unbiblical idea that a counselor can know another individual's inner person and motives, permit them to spiritualize the symptoms and to presume cure through their counseling. The following is excerpted from that chapter of our critique of *CTHC*.[2]

As we reveal in this chapter, Scott and Lambert teach that, if there are no objective biological markers, a biblical counselor can be assured that mental-emotional-behavioral symptoms are spiritually driven. This unneeded erroneous view, which should be unheeded, is the lynchpin for their house-of-cards theory about what constitutes "organically generated difficulties" in contrast to "nonmedical problems." The mental illness lynchpin is pulled by a scientific exposé of its fallacious foundation and correspondingly their house of cards comes tumbling down. More serious than the scientific evidence against their mental illness view is their audacious assumption that they can know what only the Lord can know: the inner motivation and source of a behavior, whether or not it is spiritual.

The ten cases are predicated on no medical illness being found through a complete physical exam with the accompanying assumption that the mental-emotional-behavioral symptoms are, thereby, surely spiritual. These ten cases serve as a model for other biblical counselors to read and follow after their counselees have had a complete medical exam that reveals no bodily illness related to the mental symptoms. The worst part of Scott and Lambert's fallen house-of-cards mental illness idea is what is communicated to other biblical counselors, who will follow their lead because of the example established by ten highly educated, well-known, respected, and popular leaders of the biblical counseling movement (BCM).

In Chapter 1 of *CTHC*, Heath Lambert favorable quotes Jay Adams, who says:

> Organic malfunctions affecting the brain that are caused by brain damage, tumors, gene inheritance, glandular or chemical disorders, validly may be termed mental illnesses. But at the same time a vast number of other human problems have been classified as mental illnesses for which there is no evidence that they have been engendered by disease or illness at all…. [The problem with the "mentally ill"] is autogenic; it is in themselves…. Apart from any organically generated difficulties, the "mentally ill" are really people with unsolved personal problems.[3] (First ellipsis and brackets Lambert's, second ellipsis ours, p. 8.)

Later Lambert says: "Biblical counselors believe that Christians possess everything necessary to help people with their nonmedical problems (2 Pet 1:3-4)" (p. 13, bold added).

The statements by Adams and Lambert and similar ones by others imply that one can determine whether a person has "organically generated difficulties" or "nonmedical problems" and thereby lead many biblical counselors to conclude that all one needs to do is to recommend that a counselee have "a complete physical exam" (pp. 65, 97, 150, 177, 299). Referring the counselee to a physician is often one of the counselor's "first steps" (p. 214).

Serious errors result from this type of reasoning. First is the **mistaken idea** that one can know whether or not mental symptoms that are not clearly "caused by brain damage, tumors, gene inheritance, glandular or chemical disorders" are actually "nonmedical problems." One of the most difficult health issues to deal with is the cause and treatment of mental disorders. There are numerous varieties of such disorders as the ones mentioned in *CTHC*: "schizophrenia, sexual abuse, eating disorders, bipolar" and "dissociative identity disorders," as well as depression. The big question is whether such "hard cases" are in any way "organically generated difficulties" or "nonmedical problems." The sum and substance of the *CTHC* mistaken assumption is as follows: Unless there are proven biological diseases that can account for the usual symptoms of mental disorders, **the root causes and cures are spiritual and can be resolved biblically**. Lambert says it succinctly elsewhere: "Receiving a full medical work-up allows us to rule out organic issues."[4]

Since we cannot always know whether or not there are "organically generated difficulties," **one should**

never conclude that the mental disorders are **spiritually driven,** thereby **only** needing biblical remedies. We quickly add that those with life issues, whether "organically generated" or not, should be ministered to biblically as the occasion arises.

We referred to the *Diagnostic and Statistical Manual of Mental Disorders* (*DSM-5*) earlier and the need for a warning about psychotropic medications. Here we explain why the nearly 300 mental disorders listed in the *DSM-5* qualify for biblical counseling according to the standards set forth in *CTHC.* The main reason is that nearly all these mental disorders are based upon subjective reports by the clients because there are no obvious or clear organic, physical origins to support the diagnoses.

According to a major theme of *CTHC,* biblical counselors can counsel all but the "rare exceptions" because "there are no objective biological measures for mental illness." The *CTHC* belief is that, aside from these "rare exceptions," the *DSM-5* mental disorders are not, so far as currently known, "organically generated difficulties" and are therefore "nonmedical problems." This means they surely have spiritual roots and can be resolved biblically. **To what extent a symptom is fully the result of a spiritual issue is known only to God and should not be presumed to be known by mere humans.**

Scott and Lambert, as well as others in the BCM, are woefully naïve about the biological possibilities of the very "Hard Cases" they claim to cure. E. Fuller Torrey, MD, a research psychiatrist says, "Psychiatric disorders can be caused by genetic, infectious, metabolic, and other organic etiologies, some of which are detectable by

a physical exam and blood tests, but **many cannot be**"
(bold added).[5]

Most competent practicing medical doctors who see
patients regularly and any book written by a capable
medical doctor on this subject will debunk this extremely erroneous idea and medical illness position of *CTHC*.
For example, Erno Daniel, MD, PhD, an internal medicine doctor who has been at a large medical clinic for 30
years and seen patients on a regular basis, has written a
book titled *Stealth Germs in Your Body*. In his chapter
"What Else Could It Be?" he has a section titled "We
Found Nothing" versus "There Is Nothing." Daniel says:

> Clearly there is a difference between "we found
> nothing (abnormal)" and "there is nothing (ab-
> normal)." In general "we found nothing, so far"
> means that the screening examinations and tests
> that were ordered to look for particular condi-
> tions yielded negative results at the time they
> were done. In other words, nothing truly ab-
> normal was found on the examination or on the
> tests that were chosen to be performed thus far.
> Clearly, that doesn't prove conclusively that you
> are not harboring stealth germs in your body, as
> there **is no foolproof test that can find every-
> thing**. The absence of a large number of possible
> conditions does not exclude the presence of some
> other previously undetected or evolving condi-
> tion (bold added).[6]

Daniel later explains why exhaustive testing is not
done in a section titled "Cost-benefit Considerations in
Testing." He says:

Most likely, you were only tested for conditions that were suspected to be causing your symptoms, and conditions for which there is specific effective treatment available. One of the main reasons why tests for many "nontreatable" conditions are not routinely ordered is because ethical doctors try not to incur unnecessary expenses. Although information obtained from some tests might be interesting, the tests usually won't be ordered if the results are not expected to yield direct benefit in correcting or managing your condition as demonstrated by evidence-based medical practices.[7]

Anyone reading the entire chapter of Daniel's book would see the reasons why one cannot rule out a medical condition when a complete physical finds nothing and why **Scott and Lambert's mental illness theme is a mental illness myth**. When there are no objective biological markers no one, no matter how expert, educated, and experienced in the field of medicine, can say for sure whether or not there are "organically generated difficulties" involved or whether they are "nonmedical problems."

In *Scientific American Mind*, an article titled "Ruled by the Mind" says, "Many common ailments and physical conditions can influence the brain, leaving you depressed, anxious or slow-witted." The article discusses some somatopsychic disorders in which "the root of the problem [mental disorder] lies in the body—and in particular the immune system."[8] There are many bodily disorders that doctors do not relate to the mental symptoms that result from them. An article in the *Wall Street*

Journal titled "Confusing Medical Ailments With Mental Illness" refers to "more than 100 medical disorders" that "can masquerade as psychological conditions or contribute to them, complicating treatment decisions." The article states, "Recognizing an underlying medical condition can be particularly difficult when there is also a psychological explanation for a patient's dark moods."[9] Think about the possible prolific personal harm that can result from assuming a spiritual cause and biblical cure for the nearly 300 mental disorders listed in the *DSM* as can often happen with the "Hard Cases" counseled by biblical counselors!

A whole range of bodily disorders have mental symptoms. Some of these biological disorders are in their embryonic stages—not yet detectable. These symptoms can result in mental disorders that would be diagnosed by biblical counselors as spiritual problems requiring biblical solutions. There is a whole class of diseases called "idiopathic." According to the dictionary, "Idiopathic is an adjective used primarily in medicine meaning *arising spontaneously* or *from an obscure or unknown cause.*"[10] In other words, there are no biological markers for such diseases; there are only symptoms. There are many such diseases of the body and brain that occur, and we assume that biblical counselors would have to agree that there are idiopathic diseases of the body that are known only by their symptoms. In essence, biblical counselors are saying, "No discernible biological, bodily markers means no biological, bodily problems." Just as diagnosing **idiopathic bodily diseases** that lack biological markers must rely upon symptoms, diagnosing **idiopathic brain**

diseases that lack biological markers must also rely upon symptoms.

What about true bodily or brain disorders or **diseases yet to be discovered**, whose symptoms are mental, emotional, or behavioral? As we noted earlier, there are all sorts of mental disorders that have been treated in the past by psychiatrists as psychological disorders that later were found to have physical causes. Because "organically generated difficulties" were not found at the time, those disorders would have been diagnosed as psychological by psychologists, but spiritual by biblical counselors, needlessly and foolishly foisting unneeded, unhelpful, and sometimes dangerous counseling regimens on unsuspecting counselees.

Just as there may be **no biological markers** that clearly reveal the etiology of various mental disorders there are also **no spiritual markers** for them. In regard to spiritual markers, all of them are symptomatic, e.g., church membership, personal testimony, words, actions, financial giving, teaching, Christian family, Bible college or seminary degree, being a pastor, etc., none of which can be said to be a certain sign that one is a believer. It is as serious an error to assume that those with mental disorders without biological markers are suffering exclusively for spiritual reasons as it is to assume that those with mental disorders with biological markers are suffering exclusively for biological reasons. How sad it is when a Christian attempts to diagnose a fellow believer's mental disorder as spiritually caused when, indeed, there may be hidden biological reasons for the symptoms. There should be no spiritual diagnosing to begin with! The Bible does not support the idea of one believer analyzing another believer's heart and then diagnosing his spiritual condition. As we said earlier, that only leads to guesswork since only God knows the inner person.

To be fair-minded one needs to avoid categorically placing individuals who are without biological markers into either a spiritual or a medical box because only God knows the nature and extent of each. Beyond the obvious cases, such as brain tumors, etc., the ones who are biologically afflicted but do not have biological markers are known only by God. Only God knows for sure when biological markers are absent whether there is a spiritual or biological cause and whether a spiritual or medical solution is all that is necessary. And, only God knows who is truly saved.

In the absence of biological markers, spiritualizing a mental disorder and prescribing a biblical regimen alone can be a serious a mistake, because **counseling based on such wrong assumptions could induce guilt and greater suffering** even for the most godly individuals, especially if there is no change in symptoms. It is much better to admit that one does not know what underlies an individual's mental-emotional-behavioral symptoms and yet provide spiritual helps to hopefully alleviate the suffering and promote spiritual growth. Everything in life has spiritual overtones. However, an illness is not necessarily the result of spiritual choices and that includes mental disorders, which can be the result of genetics, hormones, diseases, injuries, and circumstances, all of which can affect one's state of mind.

Believers will respond to the challenges of life more and more biblically as they grow in the spirit and mature in the faith. Therefore, one should seek to minister the things of the Spirit and build individuals up in the Word. Whether the problem is biological, spiritual, or both, believers may minister God's mercy, grace, and truth to fellow believers, because every occasion of suffering can be used for comfort and spiritual growth—unless the one who ministers thinks he can diagnose another person's heart attitude. There must be much humility in personally ministering to those who are suffering, even if they have brought this suffering upon themselves.

Let's say a woman who is suffering from a mental disorder is not a believer. Let's say by the mercy and grace of God she is converted, but her mental disorder remains. In such cases, **some** may be delivered from mental disorders. However, others, because of biological impairment, known or not yet discovered, will continue to suffer as long as the body/brain is affected. Yet, during that time a believer who continues in depression may draw close to the Lord and find comfort and encouragement in time of need. While the authors of *CTHC* may wonderfully bring forth the use of Scripture, they woefully leave their readers in danger of suffering from mental symptoms believing that their current spiritual life is causing these distressing symptoms and is responsible for their current state of mind and that, as soon as they grow spiritually, their mental disorder will be over. This will surely cause many such believers to feel guilty about their own "spiritual lack" when they may be as spiritually sound as the authors of *CTHC* themselves. *CTHC* is a great discredit to those godly individuals and a great disservice to the church.

Often times only God knows if the mental disorder is caused in whole or in part by a spiritual problem, and therefore only God truly knows if a spiritual solution is all that is necessary. The biblical counselors' conclusion that a mental disorder is spiritual under the conditions they set encroaches upon God's territory. They need to repent of claiming to have knowledge that only God can truly know.

Logical Fallacy

Biblical counselors are probably unaware of the fact that they are involved in an either/or logical fallacy. One logic book describes the either/or fallacy s follows:

> The *either/or* fallacy, sometimes called *false dichotomy*, consists of mistakenly assuming that there are only two possible solutions to some problem or that solving some problem consists of choosing between only two alternatives. The argument moves by showing that one of the alternatives is false or unacceptable and concludes that the other must be true.[11]

Based upon their naiveté about true diseases and their bogus either/or fallacy of true diseases and spiritual disorders, biblical counselors rush in "where angels fear to tread" to counsel individuals for whom no true bodily or brain disease has been found. It may never have occurred to them that **a mental disorder could be the result of a combination of a true disease and a spiritual disorder or a true disease not discovered during a complete medical examination.**

Mental Illness Confusion

Mental symptoms can be related to a person's spiritual life, but to categorically say that it is either physical or it is spiritual is just plain wrong reasoning. There are many other bodily symptoms that consistency would demand that they be labeled spiritual disorders when no physical disease can be found. Backaches resulting in mental symptoms are frequent complaints that often escape a specific disease diagnosis to relate them to the brain. Are those backaches spiritual problems? Likewise for sinus and respiratory disorders that result in mental symptoms where no true disease is found to connect the two—are these spiritual problems? And what about the controversial disorders of fibromyalgia and chronic fatigue, with doctors arguing on both sides of the body/mind issue? Also, how about headaches related to mental disorders where all the possible medical testing has been done, but the headaches persist? Since they affect the brain absent any biological markers, are these spiritual problems as well? What do biblical counselors do with the fact that women have "twice the risk of depression as men"[12] and two-thirds of those with General Anxiety Disorder are women?[13]

Furthermore, brain imaging is still in its early stages of usefulness in diagnosing mental disorders. Certain problems, such as cell damage through tumors, strokes, and other mishaps, can be identified through brain imaging. But other activities in the brain having to do with neurotransmitters vary during the day and from day to day so that a specific diagnosis through brain imaging is definitely limited. Disease can be extensive, but not identifiable. Some diseases can be rampant and horrible but not even known. Therefore, it is worse than naïve to state definitively that mental problems that cannot be seen through existing medical tests, no matter how thorough, are spiritual problems.

A recent article indicates that the "first blood test to diagnose major depression in adults has been developed."[14] Prior to this there was no such medical marker. Without knowing about this recent discovery and thus assuming the problem is spiritual, Scott and Lambert and other BCM counselors would assume the depression to be solely a spiritual problem if nothing is found in the usual "complete physical exam." Through the years the list of true diseases has expanded and will continue to expand as more cause and effect relationships are discovered. Many disorders labeled "psychological" by the psychotherapists and "spiritual" by biblical counselors may be identified in the future as true diseases resulting in mental, emotional, or behavioral symptoms, thus bringing embarrassment to those who follow this foolishness.

Some diseases creep in subtly, and some, which can cause mental symptoms in their early stages, are not identified for years. Because of the limitations of a physical exam, no matter how extensive, one may never know for sure if the mental symptoms have a physical base. Leaping to a conclusion that it is a spiritual problem, as with an either-or fallacy (bodily or spiritual), after a complete physical that reveals nothing, is naïve at best and cruel at worst when put into practice.

There are many examples we could provide from our own ministry experience and from other testimonies of overlooked physical causes of mental disorder symptoms. There are two cases of Christian women, with whom we are personally acquainted, who were diagnosed with psychiatric disorders because no known physical disease was discovered even after numerous physical tests and examinations by a variety of doctors. Both women were diagnosed as having a psychiatric disorder. In the first case, it was suggested that the woman's husband might possibly be involved in her disorder. After several years of struggling, she was finally found to be a victim of Lyme disease, which is caused by a deer tick. The second woman reported a number of psychiatric symptoms and was diagnosed with schizophrenia. Months later, after she had continued to suffer from the various symptoms, an astute doctor revealed that her symptoms were due to a viral pathogen. Can you imagine the damage the biblical counselors could cause with these two Christian women and many others?

During the period of time prior to the discovery of Lyme disease in the one and the virus in the other, with accompanying psychiatric symptoms in both, these two women would probably have been labeled as having spiritual problems by the biblical counseling standards. They would probably tell these two women who had thorough physical examinations by a variety of doctors, "Your mental problems are simply spiritual problems that we can diagnose and treat biblically, because no 'organically generated difficulties' have been found." After the discovery of their true diseases, the biblical counselors would be regarded as false teachers.

Conclusion

Just as psychological counseling and psychotropic drugs have been erroneously used over the years when no biological illness has been found, many biblical counselors now mistakenly assume that sin or lack of faith or some other possible spiritual defect is the cause of problems when no "organically generated difficulties" are found. Just because no "organically generated difficulties" are found **does not mean that none exist.** Just because there is no known cause and effect relationship between the brain/mind and many of the mental disorders does not mean that one will not eventually be found. When more becomes known about the brain and its affect on the mind/body and about how various brain activities can affect thinking, feeling, and even behaving, these new discoveries will make fools of those who have been following the either/or fallacy and concluding that the mental disorders are for certain spiritually caused.

We must all be open to the possibility that some of the metaphorically speaking mental illnesses will have known organic causes in the future. The brain, because of its enormous complexity, can have things organically wrong with it that cause mental-emotional-behavioral symptoms. Even though these ten biblical counselors are attempting to analyze and diagnose spiritual conditions, they rely mostly on psychiatric terms and psychological labels, such as "schizophrenia, sexual abuse, eating disorders, bi-polar," and "dissociative identity disorder" as well as depression, as they flaunt their contrived counseling victories. Such labels are unnecessary when ministering God's love in mercy and truth according to His Word and by His Spirit.

Many of God's people have difficult decisions to make. Many have taken the full physicals provided by their clinics and recommended by biblical counselors. They have waited months with mental symptoms. They have painfully gone to work at times and stayed home at other times, doing the best they could under the prevailing, painful symptoms. Their loved ones have perhaps drawn alongside and helped to bear the awful burden of those so afflicted. No one should add to their burden through the use of an either/or fallacy resulting in spiritual blame that does not fit the facts or history.

The best, most sensible position for a Christian to take, even after a complete physical examination that reveals nothing, is neither to imply nor state that a mental symptom is necessarily due to a spiritual problem. But, regardless of whether a brain disorder is a spiritual or biological problem, **the correct thing to do**, in addition to any other medical treatment that may be necessary and helpful, **is to minister biblically without attempting to spiritually analyze or diagnose a fellow believer.**

There is always a place for biblical encouragement, counsel, and even rebuke, but such should be done in great humility (Gal. 6:1-3) and with consideration for the possibility of biological involvement. Sometimes the best one may say is, "I don't have a clue, but God knows, and He is faithful to His promises to be with His children (Heb. 13:5), to enable them to endure trials (Phil. 4:13), and to use all for their good (Rom. 8:28-29)." Christians who desire to minister to fellow believers should beware of the temptation of becoming like Job's counselors—adding to a person's pain through fallacious conclusions based upon no "organically generated difficulties" or "medical problems" existing followed by condemnation by spiritualizing the causes for nearly all of the 300 mental disorders in the *DSM* plus any others where no apparent objective biological markers appear.

9

Sinful

Counseling

Most counseling, whether psychological or biblical, is problem centered and therefore most often sinful in its approach. In seeking to find reasons behind a person's problems, such counseling often involves sinful conversations in which the faults and failings of others are explored as a means of help. In fact, after seeing, hearing, and reading many counseling cases done by psychological and biblical counselors, we conclude that both psychological and biblical counseling are typically sinful environments in that they violate Scripture.

Corrupt Communication

Words are powerful and revealing. James describes the power of words in the human tongue:

> If any man offend not in word, the same is a perfect man, and able also to bridle the whole body.... And the tongue is a fire, a world of iniquity: so is the tongue among our members, that it defileth the whole body, and setteth on fire the course of nature; and it is set on fire of hell....

> But the tongue can no man tame; it is an unruly evil, full of deadly poison. (James 3:2b, 6, 8.)

Words can carry great destructive power. A few unkind words can ignite a battle between persons, groups, and countries. Words can be poison to the soul, both of the speaker and hearer. The fire kindled by the tongue can start with a spark of talebearing, which can lead to misunderstanding, ill feelings, acrimony, animosity, bitterness, and the destroying of other people's privacy to the point of growing into a wildfire. The Bible is clear that the control of one's tongue is a barometer of spiritual maturity. Of course controlling the tongue would shut down almost all psychological and biblical counseling!

Our Journey

Many years ago we traveled through the dark terrain of psychology hoping to discover the secrets of human nature and how to help people suffering from problems of living. After six university degrees between us, with one being a doctorate in educational psychology, the two of us concluded that psychotherapy was a **hoax** being perpetrated on the American public. The doctorate in educational psychology from the University of Colorado qualified one of us for the Clinical Psychologist license in California, which was never applied for. Some years later the president of the Association for Humanistic Psychology, Dr. Lawrence LeShan, said: "Psychotherapy may be known in the future as the greatest hoax of the twentieth century."[1] Worse yet, the theories and therapies of counseling psychology may eventually be recognized as one of the greatest heresies of modern-day Christianity.

The more we searched through the theories and therapies of counseling psychology, the more we saw its fallacies, failures, and false ways. It was not until the bright light of the Gospel shined in our lives that we saw hope for mankind and the true answer to problems of living! Our confidence in the conversation of counseling to help people solve problems of living shifted from the psychological way to what we thought was the spiritual way. We became part of the biblical counseling movement until we realized that in many ways it simply reflected the psychological way.

In 1985 Moody Press published our book titled *How to Counsel from Scripture*. At that time we were an active part of the biblical counseling movement. However, just a few years later, we discovered what those in the biblical counseling movement were actually doing during their counseling. Thus, we departed from the movement and asked Moody Press to put the book out of print because of the various ways in which it supported the biblical counseling movement (BCM).

As we looked more deeply into the movement, we could see that it incorporated the same kinds of sinful conversations as the psychological counseling movement. To explain our concerns and the reasons for departing from the BCM, we wrote *Against "Biblical Counseling": For the Bible*.[2] Since then we have extensively written material revealing that the literal counseling conducted by the leaders of the BCM fails when examined biblically. We have exposed the veiled truth that the biblical counseling leaders are in biblical error, as they have imbibed from the polluted streams of the psychological counseling format in their integration, eclecticism, and pragmatism.

In spite of the numerous psychological theories and therapies and biblical approaches, both psychological and biblical counseling are problem-centered and work towards seeking insight into and resolution of the problems being addressed. By following this psychological format of problem solving, both psychological and biblical counseling approaches violate Scriptural admonitions and prohibitions regarding human relationships and verbal communication. The counselor and counselee are looking in the wrong direction. They are looking at outside influences and reasons rather than at the cross of Christ by which those who believe are changed inside and out.

Such a problem-centered approach supports a victim mentality, often blames parents and others in both past and present circumstances, and ends up being filled with sinful communication and self-justification. Thereby the flesh or the old nature becomes strengthened. Then, as it is strengthened, the individual may never see the desperate need for salvation or the great possibilities for spiritual growth. Such counseling truly looks like a satanically inspired hoax, as it easily draws people towards operating according to the flesh.

Many individuals who have desired to help others become biblical counselors, follow the leaders of the BCM, and use this sin-laden problem-centered approach. Even as they use Scripture along the way, they unwittingly feed the flesh rather than the spirit. Although their use of Scripture may indeed be instructive and have some salutatory effects because of the power of the Word, their use of Scripture does not sanctify this problem-centered procedure. Instead, **centering on problems invariably results in conversations that violate Scripture**.

"Hidden in Plain Sight"

We all know the expression "hidden in plain sight." The idiomatic definition is "seemingly hidden, but actually not hidden and easy to find." If one pays attention to what is actually said in either psychological or biblical counseling, one would clearly see that counseling conversations are sinful. They are "in plain sight," but a counseling mind-set blinds most people from this obvious "in plain sight" nature of counseling. From its very beginning, counseling has depended on people looking for answers to their problems in what others have either done to them or not done for them. The process of the search involves talking about others in their absence and much of this talk is simply sinful. Parents, spouses and others are often dishonored and even denigrated.

There is some good biblical material in the various biblical counseling manuals, books, and certificate and degree programs. However, as we have said all along, the major undoing of the biblical counseling movement is found in their literal counseling and case studies. This is their Achilles heel! The good biblical material is undone by their live counseling, which reveals what they actually do. There are thousands of biblical counseling books, videos, and audios, but not many have literal cases with detailed dialogue. The best way to recognize the **unbiblical nature of biblical counseling** that explores personal relationships is to read or hear and evaluate available literal, live (not simply playacted) counseling by using biblical standards. There one can see and hear how the counseling problems are discussed and what sinful conversations are actually involved. They are similar to psychological counseling in that they are **heavily problem-centered in the most unbiblical ways and often involve sinful speaking**.

Why are those involved in counseling, as counselor or counselee, blind to what is in plain view? Have they simply overlooked, ignored, denied, or justified the sinful content of their conversations? One reason may be the current mind-set, both outside and inside the church, which is this: "How can anyone be helped without talking about their problems, past and present circumstances, and all the people involved?" This very mind-set has blinded even those who should have a clear vision and may have clear vision in other areas. Even those who see glimpses of what is in plain sight may ignore the evidence for pragmatic reasons.

Over the years we have exposed sinful aspects of both psychological and biblical counseling. However, the practitioners and participants, blinded to what is "hidden in plain view," continue to support the status quo. Instead, they should be examining and practicing all the ways that Scripture gives, without resorting to evil speaking and breaking commandments having to do with relationships.

Through the years we have taken all the literal live counseling sessions of the leaders of the BCM that we could find and examined every word, every sentence, every expression, every emotion in the light of Scripture. We conclude that their counseling is contrary to the admonitions, prohibitions, and restrictions of the Word of God and is therefore sinful. This is clearly revealed in much of our writings, including our books *Person to Person Ministry, Counseling the Hard Cases: A Critical Review; Stop Counseling! Start Ministering!* and *Biblical Counseling Reviews*, which includes an appendix that lists a number of Bible verses that are most often violated by both psychological and biblical counselors. In this chapter we will review some of the evidence for those who want to see what is "hidden in plain sight."

Scriptural Violations in Problem-Centered Counseling

In truly Bible-based ministry there would be no talebearing, inappropriate (often sinful) discussions (as in marriage counseling), blaming the past, playing the victim, or dishonoring parents, as described in the following sections. Thankfully there is the exceptional person who accepts responsibility for the problem and seeks advice as to what to do in accordance with God's Word. However, practically speaking, almost every person and couple in counseling want to describe the problem and have it fixed quickly to their satisfaction. Although the leaders of the biblical counseling movement would agree that all such admonitions, prohibitions, and restrictions of Scripture should be obeyed and not violated, they overlook, allow, and even encourage these kinds of sinful speaking in their counseling! The live, literal counseling of the biblical counselors we have heard and seen reveals these serious violations of God's Word.

Although there are many other violations of Scripture that often occur during problem-centered counseling, here we focus only on talebearing, inappropriate (often sinful) discussions (such as in marriage counseling), blaming the past, playing the victim, and dishonoring parents, all of which are examples of sinful behavior.

Talebearing

What do people talk about in counseling? They talk about themselves, their feelings, their relationships, their problems, and other people in their lives. In problem-centered counseling people often talk about their parents, spouse, children, other relatives, and close friends, as well as numerous other people. What might they be saying? More often than not, the counselee will talk about people who are not present. While there may be no intentional lying, the story will be told from the teller's perspective, with details chosen from the teller's memory. And because of the nature of memory, the story is rarely an exact replica of the events. Therefore, it often turns into a tale that places the teller in a better light than the others being talked about.

Problem-centered counseling encourages talebearing. Quite often the very act of individual or group counseling will involve participants saying personal things about other people who are not present. That often involves talebearing—spreading gossip, secrets, biased impressions, and so forth about others who are not present. In fact, counseling often encourages such talebearing as the counselor elicits details and continually searches for clues as to the whys and wherefores of what is troubling the individual. After all, most problems of living involve other people.

When we warn about gossip and dishonoring, we do not condone covering up actual serious sins that may have been committed, but those would have to be verified, not just talked about in counseling. If an actual crime has been committed, one should report the crime to the civil authorities, not just talk about it in counseling.

What the Bible Says

The Bible warns us about the evil of talebearing: "The words of a talebearer are as wounds, and they go down into the innermost parts of the belly" (Proverbs 18:8; 26:22); "He that goeth about *as* a talebearer revealeth secrets: therefore meddle not with him that flattereth with his lips" (Proverbs 20:19); "Where no wood is, there the fire goeth out: so where there is no talebearer, the strife ceaseth" (Proverbs 26:20). Moreover, the Lord commands His people not to act as talebearers: "Thou shalt not go up and down as a talebearer among thy people" (Lev. 19:16).

Complaining about other people during counseling will generally give a very biased view. As the counselor hears the ongoing complaints, she cannot help but form an impression of the person being complained about. The counselor is hearing only one side of the story and would tend to see the situation from that perspective.

When talebearing includes false information about another person, it becomes bearing false witness. "Thou shalt not bear false witness against thy neighbour" (Exodus 20:16; see also Deut. 5:20; Ps. 101:5; Prov. 24:28). Bearing false witness in counseling can happen as a person describes situations from a hurt and biased perspective. Sometimes a person is covering his own sin by exaggerating the sins of others and finding fault in areas that would not even be considered sinful, such as annoying habits. Tainted tales about other people are grievous. Proverbs 25:18 says, "A man that beareth false witness against his neighbour is a maul, and a sword, and a sharp arrow."

How many counselors actually check out the details of the stories they have been told? Very few, if any. In fact, recovered memory counselors contend that it is their duty to believe and support the counselee, even though research has demonstrated that memory is faulty and that counselees lie to their counselors. Many counselees deceive by telling only part of the story and thereby turn it into talebearing. The Bible advises getting the facts before believing the tales: "He that is first in his own cause seemeth just; but his neighbour cometh and searcheth him" (Prov. 18:17).

Inappropriate (often sinful) Discussion (such as in marriage counseling)

With certain exceptions, it is sinful to discuss marital problems with others or to complain about one's spouse to someone in each other's presence or absence (Eph. 5:21, 22, 25; Prov. 18:17). She talks about him when he's not there; he talks about her when she's not there; or they talk about one another in front of the counselor. In problem-centered counseling counselors not only listen to ongoing complaints, but often encourage such expression and ask for more.

Personal or marital problem-centered counseling encourages one to expose sins, secrets, or private matters of others not present and is often dependent on talebearing. If a woman complains about her husband in counseling or elsewhere, she is often revealing private matters, exposing perceived or actual faults, and/or making him seem worse than he really is. If a husband complains about his wife in counseling, or elsewhere, he is very possibly revealing private matters, exposing perceived or actual faults, and/or making her seem worse than she really is. Talebearing harms relationships and may be one of the main reasons marriage counseling so often leads to divorce. Those who love one another will rarely share private matters about their spouse with others, including counselors.

Violating the One Flesh of Marriage

Marriage provides many opportunities for spiritual growth. But instead, couples in counseling tend to blame each other and want the other partner or circumstances to change. Instead of seeking the Lord to work in their own lives, they go to problem-centered counseling, talk about their problems, and expect the counselor to do something (change circumstances or the other partner). Quite often people want the counselor to help the other partner see their point of view. If the counseling does not fix the problems, the people feel they have done everything they can, figure there is no hope for change, and move into the direction of separation and/or divorce—all at the expense of their precious children's well-being. What does the Bible say?

> Submitting yourselves one to another in the fear of the Lord (Eph. 5:21).

> Wives, submit yourselves unto your own husbands, as unto the Lord (Eph. 5:22).

> Husbands, love your wives, even as Christ also loved the church, and gave himself for it (Eph. 5:25).

These are commands, not simply suggestions or advice. Based on these verses, we conclude that the following problem-centered counseling activities violate the biblical one-flesh principle:

1. Discussing marital problems with others or complaining about one's spouse in each other's presence. If a husband is loving his wife as Christ loves the church, he will not be exposing her weaknesses and failures to others (including the children). If the wife is honoring her husband, submitting to him (as the church to Christ) and loving him (Titus 2:3-4), she will not be exposing his weaknesses and failures to others (including the children). Of course, there are necessary exceptions, such as physical or sexual abuse in a family or such sins as pornography, illegal drug use, or drunkenness, which should be brought to the attention of the church leadership, and in cases where civil laws have been broken need to be brought to the attention of civil authorities.

2. Discussing marital problems with others or complaining about one's spouse in his/her absence. Proverbs 18:17 says, "He that is first in his own cause seemeth just; but his neighbour cometh and searcheth him" (Prov. 18:17). Very often one spouse will attempt to get a counselor or friend to see a situation from that perspective by talking about the other spouse in his/her absence. The one who is first to state the case may gain support from the counselor or friend, but the truth may be revealed later. Furthermore, this can lead to a further rift in the marriage relationship. It ends up being the kind of gossip that separates people. Proverbs 17:9 advises, "He that covereth a transgression seeketh love; but he that repeateth a matter separateth very friends."

3. Discussing marital problems with others for the purpose of getting a spouse to change. If people are in a personal conflict with another person and believe that it is primarily the other person's fault, they are wasting a valuable opportunity if they are trying to change the other person or simply hoping for the other person to change. Such conflict can be an exceptional opportunity for spiritual growth. If one's eyes are on the other person and that person's need for change, one can get bogged down and waste the opportunity for personal spiritual growth.

Blaming the Past

Blaming the past is one of the major themes of Freudian and other insight-oriented psychotherapies. By permitting and participating in such problem-centered counseling, the biblical counselor is clearly being unbiblical. The apostle Paul did not focus on his horrific past, but said:

> Brethren, I count not myself to have apprehended: but this one thing I do, forgetting those things which are behind, and reaching forth unto those things which are before, I press toward the mark for the prize of the high calling of God in Christ Jesus. (Phil. 3:13, 14).

Of course Paul had left all self-seeking behind and was pressing forward towards fulfilling his calling: to serve God faithfully and bring many to a knowledge of the truth.

For years the counseling way of dealing with problems of living has been to talk about the problems, feelings, circumstances, and the sins of others, including family members. Because many counseling theories consider one's childhood to be the source of later problems, much time may be devoted to looking for ways that parents and other adults failed to give the child exactly what the counselee or counselor thinks the child needed at the time.

Some problem-centered counselors encourage the counselee to remember and even re-experience the past. Since recall is never truly accurate, but rather is full of gaps that must be filled in, the memory inevitably becomes altered and enhanced. The further back the memory, the greater chance for imagination to take over and the greater the inaccuracy. As these tales unfold and are emotionally experienced, they take on a life of their own and become newly created memories—tales of parents doing things they never did or failing to do what they actually did.

Turning to the past to find reasons for present problems, as often happens in problem-centered counseling, places blame on others and on circumstances rather than on one's own responsibilities and possibilities. Because of the nature of memory, remembering the past cannot be done without enhancing, embellishing, omitting, or creating details to fill in the blanks. Therefore, this is a faulty method of help because of the brain's limited ability to remember accurately and its tendency to distort.

Playing the Victim

Problem-centered counseling sets the stage for playing the victim and blaming others, instead of recognizing the deceitfulness of one's own heart. There are individuals who are truly victims, but concentrating on their victimhood has never been a beneficial means of recovering from it.

Today there is a whole culture of victimhood way beyond those who have suffered serious tragedies. One book describes America as *A Nation of Victims*. The subtitle is *The Decay of the American Character*. According to the book's description, "The plaint of the victim—*It's not my fault*—has become the loudest and most influential voice in America." The author, Charles Sykes says:

> The ethos of victimization has an endless capacity not only for exculpating one's self from blame, washing away responsibility in a torrent of explanation—racism, sexism, rotten parents, addiction, and illness—but also for projecting guilt onto others.[3]

Sykes also says, "The impulse to flee from personal responsibility and blame others seems far more deeply embedded within the American culture."[4] He explains, "Increasingly, Americans act as if they had received a lifelong indemnification from misfortune and a contractual release from personal responsibility."[5] The many counselors who are problem-centered often both hear and support the prevalent victim mentality by focusing on "felt needs" and the healing of emotional "wounds." However, victimization shifts the attention away from one's own responsibility for what is thought, said, and done; away from one's own sin; and onto the sins of others committed against them.

Dishonoring Father and Mother

Dishonoring father and mother occurs often in problem-centered biblical counseling. When looking for the source of problems in a person's upbringing, problem-centered counseling often leads a person to violate God's commandment to: "Honour thy father and thy mother: that thy days may be long upon the land which the LORD thy God giveth thee" (Exod. 20:12). Even if a person is having problems related to parents, the command to honor father and mother, repeated in Ephesians 6:2, is to be followed. This would mean not dishonoring mother and father to a "third party," especially when the parents are not there to respond (Proverbs 18:17). Contrary to Scripture, individuals are permitted and sometimes encouraged by the counselor to talk about their past and present problems perceived to be related to parents (Exodus 20:12), and the counselee may carry on, unrestrained by the counselor. Any counseling that opens the door to a person bad-mouthing parents leads to violating the Scriptural admonition to honor parents.

Much problem-centered counseling seeks to discover reasons for present problems in the past, and much time is devoted to insignificant details about how parents might have been over-protective or not protective enough, or how they might have smothered the child with too much love or not loved enough, or how the parents did this or that. Since no parent is perfect, this is fertile ground for a great deal of sinful communication. Such counseling also distorts a person's relationship with parents, because as negative things are discussed the positive things fade away until the adult child develops a strained relationship with the parents. In fact, some people, after this kind of counseling, divorce themselves completely from their parents. Problem-centered counseling has done a great disservice to parents, who are often blamed for nearly everything that is wrong in a person's life. This in itself violates the commandment to honor parents.

Is This Kind of Talk Necessary?

This kind of talk not only happens in problem-centered counseling; it is encouraged and even generated. Even Christians who write so-called case studies that may be composites of more than one case include details about relationships that they should have no business knowing, but which are expected, elicited, and encouraged in counseling. For years people have been told that it is good to talk about their problems and to share personal details about others. Talking about these things has been promoted as necessary for mental-emotional healing, even though **no** research supports that claim. Actually, some people feel worse because the problems may appear bigger after discussing and analyzing them. Once a person describes a spouse in negative terms it is difficult to see the positive qualities, because positive qualities might undermine what has been said to the counselor. Rather than the attitude about the situation improving, there is a strong possibility that the attitude may become strongly attached to the description given to the counselor. A felt need to justify one's complaints may solidify the negative report given to the counselor and lead to further deterioration in the relationship.

Is it possible to help people without the sins of others being exposed? Is it possible to help people without talebearing? Is it possible to help people without focusing on problems? (See Chapter 10.) After all, some people, especially women, may temporarily feel better after they have talked with a sympathetic listener (counselor) about problem people in their lives. But, this feeling of unburdening oneself is short-lived and, in itself, does not solve the problems. In fact, problems often get worse, because, when people repeatedly spend emotional energy thinking and talking about what bothers them about their circumstances and other people, the problems draw so much attention that what is good and right fades into the background. Even if a person does feel better knowing that someone else has heard and cared, can ongoing counseling that encourages or even allows talebearing be the right way to help someone when talebearing can be harmful and is forbidden in Scripture? If biblical violations were eliminated from ongoing, week-after-week counseling, many counselors would not know what to talk about or what to do.

Dr. Jay Adams and the Biblical Counseling Movement

Biblical counseling as conducted today is nowhere found in Scripture! Where did it come from? Biblical counseling as conducted by those in the biblical counseling movement (BCM) is newly arrived in the church, according to Dr. David Powlison, a BCM leader.[6] It followed on the heels of the psychological counseling movement as it developed in the mid-twentieth century. To show how the modern-day BCM came to be what it is today, we turn to the work of Dr. Jay Adams, who developed the current biblical counseling format in his 1970 book, *Competent to Counsel*, and thereby founded the movement. Adams set forth his methodology of counseling in his book and later wrote: "Over the past 12 years I have worked assiduously to produce a body of Literature in a field that, prior to that time, **virtually did not exist**: the field of biblical counseling"[7] (bold added). Since the day Adams birthed the BCM, it has grown phenomenally. Fifty years ago there were no formalized biblical counseling programs and no formalized biblical counseling movement. Now there is a burgeoning biblical counseling movement with numerous and varied biblical counselors offering their services to Christians spread throughout much of the church. Thus, they are multiplying the worldly effects of their sinful problem-centered copycatting of the psychological counseling movement's sinful problem-centeredness.

Where did Adams learn this kind of counseling approach, in which counselors elicit sinful conversations? In his book *Competent to Counsel*, Adams reveals that he worked one summer under Dr. O. Hobart Mowrer, who was a research professor of psychology. Adams says:

> During the summer of 1965 we worked in two state mental institutions, one at Kankakee, Illinois, and the other at Galesburg, Illinois. In these two mental institutions, we conducted group therapy with Mowrer for seven hours a day. Along with five others, I flew with him, drove with him, ate with him five days a week. I learned much during that time, and while today I certainly would not classify myself as a member of Mow-

rer's school, I feel that the summer program was **a turning point in my thinking**.[8] (Bold added.)

The turning point in Adams's thinking resulted in the **adaptation of the psychological counseling model in which sinful, problem-centered conversations become the means of cure**. Adams's psychological counseling model then became the **gold standard** for the biblical counseling that followed.

Mowrer was a behaviorist and past president of the American Psychological Association, and his counseling conversations influenced Adams both in content and orientation. Adams's pre- and post-Mowrer experiences led him to retrofit psychological problem-centered counseling conversations, which depended on data gathering, prying, probing, and thereby provoking sinful speaking, into what he named "nouthetic counseling."

The Influence of Transparency

The sinful content of biblical counseling arises from Adams's exposure to the kind of counseling that calls for transparency. Self-centered, self-biased self-exposure with its accompanying exposure of the sins, failures, and faults of others during counseling has become a psychotherapeutic requirement. Adams's use of the psychological format of transparency came out of what he experienced with O. Hobart Mowrer in 1965. The 1960s saw the rise of the encounter movement based on theories and techniques of group dynamics.

The encounter movement, as experienced by Adams under Mowrer, was a huge leap into the public undressing of persons in front of as many others as happen to be in the group. One of the basic assumptions of encounter groups is that it is emotionally beneficial to be totally transparent and open about whatever might be bothersome about self and others. In other words, "let it all hang out," meaning to be completely candid and straightforward, saying whatever you want and condemning whomever you wish, without any need to prove anything. One could say anything about anyone without restraint.

Transparency leads to deceptive feelings of intimacy, especially when the sharing majors on personal struggles with temptations and behaviors the Bible would label as sin. Such exposure can be very enticing with its focus on self. It is like a big story-telling session all about me, myself, and I and anyone else involved in my life. Sharing biased stories engenders emotional involvement in group, family, couple, and individual therapy. The therapeutic necessity of sharing personal struggles and the "sins" of others is the foundation on which the sinful conversations of counseling rest, where self is center and sinfully speaking of others is accepted and expected. In such an environment parents are dishonored and spouses denigrated. People not present to defend themselves are belittled, criticized unfairly, spoken ill of, defamed, slandered, run down, maligned, and given a bad name.

Learning the techniques for encouraging transparency in encounter groups influenced Adams's thinking. Thus, for Adams, self-exposure became a therapeutic absolute in the formation of his nouthetic counseling and set the gold standard for biblical counseling from *Competent to Counsel* in 1970 to this day. The BCM is predicated on **Adams's gold standard of transparency**, which biblical counselors follow today and which is a

sinful method of counseling. Even biblical counselors who have added variations of psychodynamic exploration of the inner person in their counseling continue to follow Adams's gold standard of transparency and problem-centeredness with its sinful conversations.

Adams's Gold Standard

Adams's gold standard is epitomized in his book *The Case of the "Hopeless" Marriage* (hereafter, *The Case*).[9] *The Case* is the *ne plus ultra* of what Jay Adams called "nouthetic counseling." It is a perfect example of the kind of counseling emulated by the biblical counseling movement. The back cover of *The Case* describes the book as follows:

> Here it is!
>
> You've heard about Nouthetic Counseling, and wondered what it's like. People have told you all sorts of things—were they correct? Now you have the opportunity to judge for yourself. What you couldn't do before, you now can do—peek behind the closed door to **see how a typical counseling case—from beginning to end—is conducted**....
>
> Written by Dr. Jay E. Adams (a pastor, counselor, and author of many books), this book is a practical illustration of God's solutions to our problems. (*Case*, back cover, bold added).

The subtitle of *The Case* explains the contents: *A Nouthetic Counseling Case from Beginning to End*. The *Case* is comprised of ten sessions of Pastor Greg counseling Bert and Sue. Adams has Pastor Greg say the following:

> Many—perhaps most—of those who call their counseling "Christian" or even "biblical" don't really counsel according to the Scriptures.... Truly biblical counseling, in contrast, grows out of and is consistent with the Scriptures **at every point** (*Case*, p. 118, bold added).

The following critique of *The Case of the "Hopeless" Marriage: A Nouthetic Counseling Case from Beginning to End* demonstrates that nouthetic counseling is not truly biblical "at every point." *The Case* has a biblical façade and some biblical content, but it is **not truly biblical "at every point**." With the amount of sinful conversations, *The Case* is seriously flawed at many points.

Bert and Sue have come to Pastor Greg for help because their marriage is falling apart (*Case*, p. 1). Bert and Sue describe their problems in the Personal Data Inventory (PDI), which is used by many in the BCM. Pastor Greg uses their answers to discuss their problems with them. He asks questions about the problems, because, as a BCM counselor, he must gather data about the problems, which is **not necessary** when one is truly biblical. The PDI and questions that follow provide many opportunities for Bert and Sue to say hurtful things about each other in front of a third party. And, indeed **the PDI and questions bring forth self-biased, unloving, sinful remarks along with blaming the spouse, justifying self, and expressing anger**, all of which are **sinful** according to the Scriptures:

A talebearer revealeth secrets: but he that is of a faithful spirit concealeth the matter. (Prov. 11:13.)

A soft answer turneth away wrath: but grievous words stir up anger. The tongue of the wise useth knowledge aright: but the mouth of fools poureth out foolishness.... A wholesome tongue is a tree of life: but perverseness therein is a breach in the spirit. (Prov. 15:1-2, 4.)

He that is first in his own cause seemeth just; but his neighbour cometh and searcheth him. (Prov. 18:17.)

A continual dropping in a very rainy day and a contentious woman are alike. (Prov. 27:15.)

An angry man stirreth up strife, and a furious man aboundeth in transgression. (Prov. 29:22.)

Let no corrupt communication proceed out of your mouth, but that which is good to the use of edifying, that it may minister grace unto the hearers.... Let all bitterness, and wrath, and anger, and clamour, and evil speaking, be put away from you, with all malice . (Eph. 4:29, 31.)

Providing a venue for such husband-wife interchange, in which they speak unkindly about each other, militates against a biblical marital relationship as described in Ephesians 5:22-33. The following are the types of problems surfaced by the couple (*Case*, pp. 71, 105, 114):

Bert:

Does not pick up his socks.

Does not take out the trash regularly.

Sue:

Unloads on Bert as soon as he comes home from work.

Does not serve meals that please Bert.

When the pastor asks Bert to tell him about the main problem in their marriage, Bert replies, "Well, we haven't been getting along for some time now. It seems that she won't let me be the head of the house. I..." At that point Sue interrupts Bert and says, "Won't let you. When did you ever try? You know full well that you..." The pastor then interrupts Sue and asks her to let Bert finish what he was saying. Then Bert says, "Well, as I was saying—before she flew into one of her tirades..." Sue interrupts again and says, "See, pastor, he can't be civil. A tirade? Hummph!" (*Case*, p. 11). Instead of bringing truth and love into the conversation, the counselor ends up being a kind of referee whose counseling rules actually enable a great deal of sinful speaking about each other. In addition to the problems they are already experiencing with each other come the wounds of criticism that are bound to sink way down (Prov. 26:22). Increased opportunities to offend one another in counseling will only make matters worse according to Proverbs 18:19.

The pastor invites Bert to continue even though he is sinfully speaking ill about his wife and exposing her faults to a third party. Bert then says, "As I was saying, every time I try to assume my duty as the head of my home, Sue undermines me. She always knows better.

She always has another way. She always contradicts me. The kids don't know who to believe" (*Case*, p. 12).

The pastor does set some restrictions on their rude and hurtful communication, such as having them speak to him instead of to each other and telling them not to exaggerate. Nevertheless, his rule actually encourages them to continue complaining about each other and allows them speak ill of one another, as long as they do not speak directly to each other. Not being allowed to speak to one another during counseling is an artificial restriction that does not prevent the sinful talk, but merely keeps things somewhat under the pastor's control. He thereby maintains his authoritative position, rather than being reduced to the sidelines during any argument that might erupt. One can easily see how the problem-centeredness of the counseling opens the door to couples breaking God's commandments to husbands and wives in Ephesians 5:22-33 and 1 Peter 3:5-10. Pastor Greg, like most counselors, thinks he needs these kinds of hurtful remarks and demonstrations of a husband attacking his wife instead of protecting her and of a wife demeaning and dishonoring the husband. Such talk is typical of marriage counseling both inside and outside the church.

When the pastor attempts to teach Bert about loving his wife, Bert responds, "It's just that if she'd listen to me, I could love her more." Then when the pastor gives biblical instruction regarding the husband to love his wife, Sue remarks, "See, I told him! He should love me by putting me first" (p. 15). This sinful talk could have been avoided if the pastor had cautioned them at the beginning about how speaking ill of one another and exposing each other's faults are the very opposite of love and respect.

At the end of the first session, Pastor Greg assigns homework. He says:

> Each of you is to compose a list of 100 or more ways that you are failing God as a person, as a husband or wife, and as a father or mother.... Write out your lists, and when you've finished draw a line and then hand the lists to one another to add anything that may be missing. **List specific things that bother you about one another** (p. 21, bold added).

This is a long list of 200 possible problems the couple has as "a person, as a husband or wife, and as a father or mother." Add this to problems already revealed in the PDI and the problems already discussed and the problem-centered counselor has the usual pile of problems to serve as fodder for future problem-centered counseling sessions riddled with sinful speaking. However, the mere listing of their gripes and failings could easily make matters worse. Listing 100 or more ways each for Bert and Sue to change is a negative and unnecessary assignment, but it does give the counselor something to talk about for the upcoming sessions.

Instead of bringing Scripture forth to guide the conversation, Pastor Greg is inviting Bert and Sue to further bite and devour each other. Scripture warns against such interchange: "But if ye bite and devour one another, take heed that ye be not consumed one of another" (Gal. 5:15). It would have been far better to suggest to Bert and Sue that each one bring back a list of things about each other for which they are thankful to the Lord. These can be a springboard away from problem-centeredness to Christ-centeredness. Moving them from their thanksgiving list to prayer, the Word, and worship would encourage them to grow spiritually, draw closer to the Lord, and thereby, in most cases, enable them to deal with their problems by walking according the Spirit. As Paul admonishes, "Walk in the Spirit, and ye shall not fulfil the lust of the flesh" (Gal. 5:16).

Although the pastor has attempted to give some good instruction along the way, the problem-centeredness of biblical counseling with its sinful speaking comes out again as Sue says to Bert, "You've never done much disciplining, Bert—I've had it all on my shoulders. You know that. Don't make it sound like you have!" (*Case*, p. 75.) Instead of helping Sue, Pastor Greg is enabling her to be a foolish woman who tears down her house (Prov. 14:1). It appears as though the whole marital relationship must be torn down in order for counselors to figure out how solve marriage problems in biblical counseling.

In response, Bert says, "Now, Sue, you know how hard I've tried, but to be honest, you also know that you always contradict what I tell them [the children] and they get confused. In time, I finally gave up" (*Case*, p. 75). Whoops! Here they are breaking Pastor Greg's rule. They are speaking to each other here instead of complaining about each other to the pastor. Worse than that, this kind of counseling majors in such self-justifying, blame-shifting remarks, as though such arguments must happen in front of the counselor in his attempt to save their marriage. There is no biblical example in Scripture of this type of counseling as practiced in *The Case*. Such repeated airing of complaints about each other and ongoing discussions about problems of living during numerous counseling sessions as in *The Case* and in most all counseling have no precedence in Scripture. Nevertheless, many in the church assume that this kind of talk is okay and even necessary in the counseling room.

The Case gives the impression that it's as easy as falling off a log to transform a troubled marriage. Pastor Greg's counseling succeeds marvelously because *The Case* is not a real case. It is made-up. It not only reads like fiction; it is fiction! In reality, marriage counseling is one of the most difficult areas to deal with because couples say hurtful things about each other in front of a third party. As more and more people have been going to marriage counseling, more and more have become divorced, and this includes professing Christians, who are divorcing at about the same rate as unbelievers.[10] In spite of all the time, money, and great expectations that counseling will help, marriage counseling only helps about half of the time, which is similar to sham treatment. One psychotherapist reported in a professional journal article that:

> Controlled outcome studies show that only about half of couples improve with treatment. And even among those who do make progress, a disheartening chunk, 30 to 50 percent, relapse within two years.[11]

We contend that the lack of success is due to the problem-centered counseling requirement for transparency, in which the counselees are expected and encouraged to reveal what is bothersome and problematic about the spouse and other family members, thereby exposing their faults, failures, sins, and shortcomings to a counselor in the presence or absence of a spouse within the counseling environment. In contrast, there are biblical ways to deal with personal failings and sinfulness without exposing the failures or sins of others. Those who minister biblically do not need to know such specifics about the problems or to necessarily offer solutions directly related to the problems.

Corrupting Biblically Defined Relationships

Discussing marital problems in one another's presence to a third party is unbiblical. This problem-centered approach in biblical counseling tends to corrupt the biblical roles of both men and women, and particularly in marital counseling.[12] Pastor Greg corrupts Bert's spiritual headship by eliciting and discussing problems in the marriage and then leading the couple to solutions. Pastor Greg corrupts Sue's role by having her submit to himself rather than to her husband. In contrast, true biblical ministry will encourage Bert and Sue to grow biblically and thus spiritually. In that way Bert will learn to obey the Lord in exercising his spiritual headship in love, and Sue will learn to submit to Bert "as unto the Lord" (Eph. 5:22-33).

Pastor Greg's counseling encourages the couple to sin in order to save their marriage. By "establishing rules: no interruptions, no **nasty** talk" (bold added), Pastor Greg has done nothing to prevent evil speaking or what he calls "nasty talk," since his only rules are against exaggeration, interrupting each other, and the two speaking directly to one another, none of which were obeyed.

(*Case*, pp. 11-13). Adams says: "You will notice that Pastor Greg has established God's Word as the standard for what will go on in counseling" (*Case*, p. 13). And yet, God's standard is violated all over the place in the problem-centered structure in which counselees are free to discard many admonitions regarding how **Christians are to speak and conduct themselves in truth and love:**

> Charity suffereth long, and is kind; charity envieth not; charity vaunteth not itself, is not puffed up, doth not behave itself unseemly, seeketh not her own, is not easily provoked, thinketh no evil; Rejoiceth not in iniquity, but rejoiceth in the truth; Beareth all things, believeth all things, hopeth all things, endureth all things. (I Cor. 13:4-8.)

Wouldn't it be better to teach about love and encourage Bert and Sue to examine for themselves in the presence of God, whether they are even willing to endure suffering for each other, to seek what is best for each other rather than for self, and work on an inner attitude of thankfulness that would help them not to be easily provoked? Ephesians 4:29 also should be taken into consideration, as it is violated right and left in counseling: "Let no corrupt communication proceed out of your mouth, but that which is good to the use of edifying, that it may minister grace unto the hearers." And what about Colossians 4:6? "Let your speech be alway with grace, seasoned with salt, that ye may know how ye ought to answer every man." And, Titus 3:2, which warns believers "to speak evil of no man, to be no brawlers, but gentle, shewing all meekness unto all men."

Counseling sessions that are made up of cruel and demeaning remarks about spouses, parents, and others fall far short of the mark, and yet it seems that no one cares. Pastor Greg has allowed and even encouraged, throughout the PDI and subsequent conversations, unedifying statements to be made by the couple about each other. Pastor Greg's counseling sessions are full of **murmuring, complaining, not showing love to the wife, and dishonoring the husband** (Prov. 12:4; 15:1; Eph. 5:33).

Although Pastor Greg does not allow them to say these things **to each other**, they are directed to say these same things to him **about each other**. This is a violation of Ephesians 5. Bert refers to Sue flying "into one of her tirades" (*Case*, p. 11). Sue says of Bert, "He blew off steam at his boss yesterday, saying a few choice words, and the boss fired him. Disgusting, isn't it?" (*Case*, p. 23). Some of the most petty things are said, such as Sue saying, "I think the second thing is his socks. He throws them on the floor at night, and I have to put them in the hamper the next morning" (*Case*, p. 36).

It is unfortunate and unbiblical that Pastor Greg in "establishing rules" says "no **nasty** talk." The word *nasty* is deplorable because the first definition of the word nasty is "physically filthy, disgustingly unclean." Like many words, the word *nasty* has less extreme meanings, but why use such a word when it could be misunderstood? Why does Pastor Greg **avoid calling such talk "sinful"?** It would have been more biblically correct for Pastor Greg to say, "no sinful talk." However, the words "sin" and "sinful" are almost totally absent in *The Case*! Pastor Greg does advise Bert to use the word *sin* when apologizing to his boss (*Case*, p. 30) and Adams refers to this as sin in his discussion (*Case*, p. 32). Pastor Greg does once refer to sin in a general way when he says, "Our sinful ways make us incompatible with God" (*Case*, p. 63).

Aside from these few instances, the words "sin" and "sinful" seem totally absent from the ten sessions in *The Case,* in spite of the fact that there are **numerous instances during the counseling where sin could be called *sin*, but was not**. In addition, Adams has an Appendix in which he lists "Some of the More Notable Ways in which Greg Brought This Case to a Successful End" (*Case* , pp. 137-142). Out of the 100 items listed by Adams, only one mentions "sinners" (#99). If one looks up the word *sin* and all of its variations in the Bible, it is certainly a major biblical doctrine and needs to be identified as such when necessary. Based upon Adams's ideal example, exemplified in *The Case*, nouthetic counseling seems to be an almost "sinless" approach. This serious omission of the word *sin* is one possible result of problem-centered counseling. Problem-centered counselors become so problem-centered that they ignore the sinfulness of their counseling conversations.

The details and the drama of Bert and Sue are brought out in nouthetic counseling. If Bert truly loved his wife as Christ loved the church and gave Himself for her (Eph. 5:25) and if Sue were submissive to her husband and honored him (Eph. 5:24), they would not be sharing their marital problems with a third party. It is entirely unnecessary and unbiblical to share their marital problems with a third party. There is a better way, a biblical way that does not require this public airing of problems, but surely resolves them if they are resolvable.

Dishonoring Mother

Another problem that comes up has to do with Bert's mother. Sue begins with, "You see, Bert's mother lives two blocks away from us. So she's always coming over to our house. When she does, she is always trying to run our lives. She comes over and tells Bert what to think and do; and most of the time he listens to her...." Sue adds, "She's a Charismatic who is always getting a 'prophetic word' to reinforce what she tells us to do" (*Case*, p. 92). Of course Bert's mother is not present to say whether or not she is trying to run their lives. Bert's mother's intent is assumed and believed. Here again they are encouraged to dishonor Bert's mother by speaking ill of her behind her back and placing her in the worst light.

Pastor Greg refers to Genesis 2:24, "Therefore shall a man leave his father and his mother, and cleave unto his wife: and they shall be one flesh," suggests that Bert go to his mother, and basically tells him what to say. It is very easy to "write a script" for someone else, but the script may not at all fit within the context of their relationship. Nevertheless Pastor Greg says:

> ... tell her in a kindly way that you are the head of a new family. Also tell her that, while happy to hear her suggestions, you will make your own decisions and not be persuaded to act as she wants simply because of who she is. And assure her that you will no longer allow any undue pressure or influence to interfere with your home life (*Case*, p. 93).

Pastor Greg's suggested words carry a pretty hot criticism of Bert's mother by indirectly accusing her of aggressively interfering in Bert's life and then having Bert tell her that he will "no longer allow" his mother to put pressure on him. What kind of authority is a son to take over his mother to say he would "not allow" her to do something? Instead of this **unwise** suggested pronouncement, Bert could simply proceed with doing what is right.

Bert rightly asks, "Wouldn't that hurt her?" Pastor Greg says:

> She shouldn't be hurt if she handles what you say as a Christian should. We don't act on the basis of whether others take offense at what we do, but on the basis of whether or not it is what God wants us to do (*Case*, pp. 93-94).

We agree with Pastor Greg that one should act "on the basis of whether or not it is what God wants us to do." However, we disagree with what he thinks God would want Bert to do. Is Greg attempting to change their circumstances by changing Bert's mother? We would also ask: why does Bert even have to tell his mother any of this, since these are his decisions for his own behavior change? Then, if she asks why he is not doing things her way, he could gently explain his responsibilities to lead his family without any implied criticism of his mother. We respect Bert's concern about the possibility of hurting his mother and would suggest that he pray about these needed changes and about how to accomplish his goal to be the head of the household in a way that would be pleasing to God and least hurtful to his mother. These are matters for drawing close to God, praying, and seeking God's wisdom.

At the next appointment, Bert tells Pastor Greg that he went to his mother and told her that, "while I would welcome advice, I would no longer allow anyone to meddle in our private affairs." Bert then says that his mother "told me off in non-Charismatic terms" (*Case*, p. 102).

The commandment is clear: "Honour thy father and thy mother" (Exodus 20:12). There was no need for Bert to confront his mother as bluntly as he did. Not only do problem-centered counselors often permit their counselees to dishonor their mothers and fathers; they often encourage and participate in the process. Those who follow Freudian psychological notions will dishonor their mothers and fathers by blaming them for their current problems. It is sinful to do so.

Where Is Love?

We conclude our review of *The Case*, which demonstrates the conversational standard that Adams set for the modern-day biblical counseling movement, by saying: Love should be the goal of personal ministry: loving God and one another. Those who minister to couples need to protect them from the kinds of sinful counseling conversations as revealed in *The Case*! which are tremendously unloving and unkind. With all the sinful speaking enabled in *The Case*, it is apparent that *The Case of the "Hopeless" Marriage* **is actually a case of hopeless counseling.**[13]

Jeremiah 17:9

Both psychological biblical counselors precipitate the sinful expressions of Jeremiah 17:9 as they **probe for problems, dig for details, and thereby conduct counselees into sinning** with their tongues in violation of many biblical prescriptions, proscriptions, admonitions, expectations, and warnings.

> The heart is deceitful above all things, and desperately wicked: who can know it? I the LORD search the heart, I try the reins, even to give every man according to his ways, and according to the fruit of his doings. (Jer. 17:9-10.)

Jeremiah 17:9 hearts contaminate problem-centered counseling as counselees are given free rein to talk about the sins of others not present, including unsubstantiated talebearing and hearsay, without being restricted, contradicted, or investigated. Because counseling is considered confidential, counselees may naturally skew their stories, which are generally filled with much unsubstantiated self-bias, gossip, and hearsay. In addition, the counselor's flesh may also be activated in a number of ways, particularly in the pride of being the "wise one" to counsel the needy one in the one-up/one-down counseling environment.

Not only can counselors be self-deceived as far as their own importance in the lives of fellow believers, but **they sin dreadfully by permitting and enabling others to sin** through their speaking. These counselors not only precipitate sinful communication through questions that elicit evil speaking; but they also provide a private place and an ear to hear corrupt conversations as they continue to pry and probe. Perhaps they would say that the end justifies the means, but when does God ask us to sin that grace may abound (Rom. 6:1)?

Women and Men in Counseling

Women in Counseling

At the beginning of the contemporary counseling era men were primarily the counselors, but women were primarily the willing and even eager victims of this male dominated psychic search that fossicked about in the regions of the mind and soul. The men are the ones responsible for formulating and peddling the forbidden fruit of counseling to their hapless women victims, who, in turn, are fertile territory for spelunking into the hidden mysteries of the mind.

From the very beginning of the talk therapy movement after World War II, the statistics always favored the preponderance of women over men as counselees. Women enter counseling as counselees because they are attracted to conversation as a means of solving problems. Thus, problem-centered conversations come naturally to them. Professional therapists in America are now predominantly women. Members of the National Association of Marriage and Family Therapists are at least two-thirds women and the percentage of women clinical psychologists is catching up.

Men in Counseling

Both psychological and biblical counselors typically usurp the man's spiritual headship by giving answers to questions men are not asking and by corralling them into strange touchy-feely pastures not of their liking. The *Psychotherapy Networker* (*PN*), a journal for psychotherapists, devoted an entire issue to "The Secret World of Men: What Therapists Need to Know." One of the *PN* therapists says, "Men more often came into therapy under pressure from someone else, frequently an unhappy spouse."[14] Psychotherapist writers for *PN* would no doubt agree with one of them who bluntly says that "even with men who know they need help is the very idea of sitting in a room, talking *out loud* about all this touchy-feely stuff; it creeps them out" (italics in original).[15] Men in counseling are often caught between the proverbial "rock and a hard place." They are yanked out of their reluctance to express the very feelings that women demand and are then criticized for expressing them. They often go into counseling wary and come out wimps. Men on the whole are either not that interested or they are repelled by the whole idea of going to counseling.

One author-therapist, Terrence Real, refers to these as "wife mandated referrals." He says, "The average man is as likely to ask for help with a psychological problem as he is to ask for directions." Real gives the reason: men do not consider counseling to be "manly."[16] This is doubly true among Christian men who are biblically knowledgeable and, by common sense, know they should not be there.

Of the total of those in counseling, the men who enter **voluntarily** are small in number. Gary Brooks, in his book *A New Psychotherapy for Traditional Men*, says, "Traditional men hate psychotherapy and will do almost anything to avoid a therapist's office." He continues, "In fact, I believe that men's aversion to therapy is so powerful that it's wise to assume that most male clients, at some level, don't want to be there."[17]

As much as men are not attracted to counseling, virtually all avenues in and out of the church force them into it. Again, counseling is a female-friendly activity, which obtains male clients mostly through intimidation, exaggerated claims, expectations of others, or coercion. Behind most men in psychotherapy or in biblical counseling is a woman, a court, an employer, a church denomination, or, as we have demonstrated elsewhere, a mission agency.

It is the problem-centered verbalization and emotional expressions that freak men out in this female-friendly counseling environment. Change the environment to a biblical ministry and make it clear what that means and the dark shadow of touchy-feely and the sense that a man has to become feminine to make it in counseling fades into the background. **Ministry rather than counseling will "level the playing field."**

Conclusion

Those churches and pastors that refer members to psychotherapists or biblical counselors must not believe in the sufficiency of Scripture for the issues of life. We repeat our challenge to those Christians who support, promote, or practice either psychological or biblical counseling: "Provide one live, literal (not enacted) psychological or biblical counseling session that does not violate Scripture." To date no one has been able to provide one for us, and every session of psychotherapy and biblical counseling we have observed has failed the test of Scripture! This is proof positive that Christians should not be involved with psychological counseling (psychotherapy). It is also proof positive that Christians should not be involved as participants or practitioners in the biblical counseling movement, whose leaders reflect the psychological counseling format. Christians who are suffering from mental-emotional-behavioral disorders, sometimes labeled as "mental illness," should be ministered to in the fellowship of believers. Such individuals usually have needs that far outweigh the time and effort that a psychological or biblical counselor can give, but that can be met within a fellowship of believers committed to mutual care.

As we have already shown, those who suffer from problems of living or mental disorders, with or without objective biological markers, can benefit from biblical ministry that does not use psychological or problem-centered biblical counseling with its sinful conversational approach. On the other hand, it is unwise, unscientific, and unnecessary to assume that mental disorders without objective biological markers are solely spiritual issues that simply need biblical solutions.

10

Christian Response to Mental Illness: Mutual Care in the Body of Christ

As we said at the very beginning of this book (Chapter 1), we would scientifically discredit the prolific, promiscuous, and popular use of the metaphor *mental illness* and later reveal that one does not always need to know the answer to the following question: Do those individuals who have a mental-emotional-behavioral disorder or who have been diagnosed with a mental illness without objective biological markers have a true disease needing medical treatment, a psychological problem needing a psychological solution, or a spiritual problem needing a biblical solution?

Our response was and still is: In **most cases** of personal ministry, it is both not possible and not necessary to know for sure whether or not such disorders or challenges are the result of an objective biological illness.

We also repeat once more: In this perilous, peculiar, and puzzling area of not truly knowing whether or not a mental-emotional-behavioral issue is biological or spiritual, one can nevertheless assume that **people are responsible for their behavior and can benefit from biblical ministry**. We, therefore, again repeat our recommendation that Christians who minister to others begin with the understanding that individuals, regardless of their mental-emotional-behavioral symptoms or designations, can be verbally ministered to, **as long as a rational conversation can take place and that the content of the conversation is undergirded by love and biblically-based.**

Prior to the rise of the psychological counseling movement, trials and tribulations of life were handled personally and/or in the family and/or in the church. As the biblical counseling movement followed and copied the psychological format of counseling (problem-centered), the mutual care of souls that ministered to individuals in the home and church was replaced with referrals to psychological or biblical counselors both in and out of the church.

Believers have a biblical responsibility to fellow believers who reach out for help. As part of a fellowship in the family of God, believers are called and equipped with the Word and the Spirit to aide fellow believers in biblical ways without violating biblical admonitions, as they are violated in the psychological and biblical counseling movements. In this chapter we discuss some of the many possibilities for ministering to fellow believers through mutual care. A first priority for personal ministry is to follow biblical guidelines for speaking and listening to one another, because sinful problem-centered conversations, discussed in the prior chapter, do not glorify God or edify one another. Once the problem-centered sinful counseling is avoided, ministry can proceed with anyone who needs help and desires to grow spiritually.

Spiritual growth is thus a primary purpose of mutual care, particularly when fellow believers are going through trials, sufferings, and various problems of living. Coming alongside to encourage spiritual growth is important during all seasons of life, but especially during the difficult times. Spiritual growth is essential for all believers from the moment of new birth until they see Christ face to face in glory. We emphasize this at the beginning of this chapter on the Christian response to mental illness, because every believer is to be included, whether they are beset with mental illness, which can be a long arduous trial, or simply enduring the usual spiritual battles between the flesh and the spirit (between the old ways and the new life in Christ). Therefore much of this chapter will be on the personal ministry of mutual care aimed at spiritual growth.

Mental Illness Mystique

The mystique surrounding mental illness has frightened away many people who could be of great help to those suffering from problems of living. Many people who want to help feel unqualified, especially if the one in need has been given a *Diagnostic and Statistical Manual of Mental Disorders* (*DSM*) label. The confusion of psychological counseling theories and therapies with science and the misnomer of *mental illness* have deceived the church beyond measure. Because of this deception, many churches have abandoned their responsibility for personal care and shunted problem-laden people off to counselors' offices. The secular emphasis on professionalism often influences pastors into thinking that they must carry the entire burden of personal care in addition to preaching, evangelizing, and teaching about sanctification. Then when they feel overburdened, they refer out rather than teaching their members to care for one another. God designed mutual care to be shared among believers coming alongside to minister encouragement and edification (Eph. 4:11-12). Each local body is called to help members of the body who need and can benefit from the personal ministry of mutual care.

Too many in the church have forgotten or ignored the fact that they are equipped with the necessary spiritual abilities to lead people out of darkness into new life and to encourage fellow believers to put off the old ways of the self and live by their new life in Jesus, whereby they can be transformed in attitudes, actions, and thoughts. As long as problems of living are seen as mental illnesses, mental diseases, or mental disorders, opportunities for spiritual growth are replaced by psychotherapy or biblical counseling with their usual sinful conversations.

As we have already indicated, one great misunderstanding among Christians is that the absence of objective biological markers for mental-emotional-behavioral disorders means that persons who are disordered have a spiritual problem that only needs a biblical solution. We have discredited this false and detrimental either/or fallacy in the previous chapters. Only God knows if and how much physical involvement is behind a person's mental-emotional-behavioral issues. Even an extended time of little or no sleep can bring on psychotic symptoms. Medical examinations are for the purpose of medical care, **not** for the purpose of deciding whether or not biblical ministry can be given. The personal spiritual ministry of mutual care should be available to all who can communicate and are willing to pursue spiritual growth.

We have continually exposed the fact that both psychological and biblical counseling are problem-centered, resulting in sinful conversations. Truly understanding the content of the preceding chapters and particular Chapter 9 will release Christians from the bondage of the status quo. It will free them to participate in mutual care in the Body of Christ as both givers and receivers by grace through faith. Paradoxically, once set free to place full trust in the Word of God, the saving work of Christ, and the sanctifying work of the Holy Spirit, one will only need to refer to Chapters 1-9 as reminders to stay the biblical course and not fall back into the ways of the world. **The challenge is to stand firm in the faith and resist sin-laden counseling conversations!**

Mutual Care versus Counseling

In addition to psychological and biblical counseling being loaded with sinful conversations, such counseling lacks a tremendous trove of valuable help that is available in the personal ministry of mutual care in a church fellowship. The limitations of one counselor, one office, one form of help (conversation), usually one 50-minute hour once a week are a stark contrast to what should be available in the Body of Christ, where all are called to love and serve one another. If the church operates according to New Testament principles, it will provide opportunities for believers to help one another in a variety of ways. Consider the great resources already in place in a local church in which believers are walking with the Lord:

Being available 24/7 is possible when the ministry is shared among believers, rather than one person having a "case load." Several different people may be involved in ministering to an individual in need.

Visiting a person at home, hospital, or work place may occur naturally as necessary because these are simply fellow believers experiencing problems of living. Neither a specified place nor restricted office hours should interfere with mutual care.

Shared meals and coffee/tea/refreshment time can be considered opportunities for fellowship and sharing both as fellow believers and as friends, where the conversations can be edifying—encouraging one another in faith instead of the corrupt communication of counseling.

Providing food, money, and such practical assistance as child or elder care, help with household chores, etc. are included in the benevolence activities of local churches. The person who ministers personally may be the one to perform these additional acts of love or they can be shared with other members of the Body of Christ.

Daily prayer for one another and opportunities to pray together personally or on the phone.

Expressions of love and care in the local fellowship, including hospitality, ongoing encouragement, and sending cards for various occasions (from congratulations to condolences).

Godly relationships in which believers are equal at the cross of Christ rather than in an artificial one-up/one-own position with the counselor in a superior position.

Relationships can continue on and develop further after the initial problems are cared for. These can be like family relationships. After all, the church is a family of believers who have the same heavenly Father.

The above are merely examples of what would be operating biblically and practically in a Bible-based fellowship. Biblically-based mutual soul care that adds hands and feet to conversations will put to shame those who offer their 50-minute relationships, filled with corrupt communication. These are all in addition to the vital worshipping and fellowshipping together.

There is also an important matter of church leadership responsibilities, which include biblical teaching, worship, and, if necessary, biblical discipline. Those who minister in the Body of Christ are under the authority and leadership of the local church. Within the context of the church there are both leadership and accountability. When Christians buy counseling services from outside centers, they do so without the leadership, protection, and accountability of a body of believers organized for the work of the ministry according to Ephesians 4:11-16.

The local church is the place for preaching and teaching and for pastoral and mutual care for the edification of all believers, under the authority of the foundation laid by Scripture and as given by Jesus Christ. It is the pastor's responsibility to equip the saints with the Word of God for the work of the ministry in all levels of mutual care. And then, as believers mature in the faith, they are further equipped for mutual care of one another. Truly biblical ministry builds up the Body of Christ through preaching, teaching, evangelizing, and caring for one another through mutual encouragement, instruction, admonition, confession, repentance, forgiveness, restoration, consolation, and comfort, as believers remind one another of what Christ has accomplished for them. When the goal is to edify, there is no room for corrupt communication, evil speaking, gossip, blame, or expressions of bitterness, unbiblical anger, or malice within pastoral or mutual care in the Body of Christ, as they often occur in the biblical counseling movement. All should be done to glorify God and nurture the spiritual growth of believers into the image of Christ, rather than to glorify counseling and empower the flesh.

The conversation of caring for one another in the Body of Christ is not a professional interchange between a so-called expert and a client or between a counselor and counselee. It is between two or more believers who are learning to walk in the Spirit and encouraging one another to do so. Biblical mutual care heavily depends on the Holy Spirit to minister the truth and application of God's Word to all involved in the conversation.

Mutual Care for Spiritual Growth

The ministry of mutual soul care cannot be reduced to formulas because it relies on the work of the Holy Spirit in a believer's life. Mutual care of the soul emphasizes spiritual growth, whereby the believer walks with the Lord according to the Spirit rather than according to the flesh. Consider the following reasons for ministry that encourages spiritual growth:

1. When believers give attention to the Lord and His Word they are enabled to grow spiritually and to better deal with problems of living. This is all through relationship with Christ as He described with the analogy of the vine and the branches in John 15:1-11.

2. God has a plan and purpose for every one of His children. He is the Potter and uses all things in a believer's life to complete the work of conforming each one to the image of Christ. (Romans 8:28-29).

3. The problems themselves can be used as catalysts for spiritual growth. See, for example, James 1:2-4 and 1 Peter 5:10.

4. Problems can serve to bring believers to the end of themselves (flesh) and make them more dependent on Christ to guide them and lead them as they take His yoke upon us (Matt. 11:28-30).

5. Problems can serve to put a person in a position to comprehend God more fully, to recognize the flesh for what it is, to abhor it, to deny self, and to seek God's will and wisdom (Job 42).

6. As believers draw close to God through trials, they will grow spiritually (1 Peter 1:6-8). Scripture gives examples of people who drew close to God in affliction and became fruitful for Him (King David, the apostle Paul, and those in the early church). See 2 Cor. 4:7-11 and 2 Cor. 12:6-10 for example.

7. Spiritual growth enables people to walk pleasing to God and to be equipped for the trials of life. This principle is woven throughout Scripture. See, for example, Ephesians 4.

8. Problems of living signal that spiritual warfare is taking place. The battle involves the world, the flesh, and the devil. As a believer recognizes and acts on the truths of 2 Cor. 10:3-6; Galatians 5:16,17; Ephesians 6:10-18; and 1 Peter 5:8-10, he will grow spiritually and learn how to deal with problems of living according to what the Lord has provided.

9. As believers recognize more of all that Christ is in them, they will gain courage for the present and hope for the future. As they learn to walk according to their life in Him, their lives will be transformed as described in Colossians 3.

10.Growing spiritually brings forth the fruit of the Spirit: "But the fruit of the Spirit is love, joy, peace, longsuffering, gentleness, goodness, faith, meekness, temperance: against such there is no law" (Gal. 5:22-23).

The goal of spiritual growth is far greater than present problem solving. The benefits so outweigh any other course of action that every believer should jump at the chance to use everything possible for spiritual growth, to be conformed to the image of Christ, and to live to the glory of God. Believers are encouraged to grow in their new life in Christ, which is spiritually alive because the Spirit of Christ lives in them. The source of the new life is God and therefore it is both spiritual and eternal. When believers are walking in the Spirit they are living by grace through faith in the Lord Jesus Christ. They are putting off the old ways of what they were before receiving His life and they are following Jesus in holiness, righteousness, truth, mercy, kindness, goodness, love, joy, peace, longsuffering, patience, humility, temperance, gentleness, faith, forgiveness, and obedience to

God. When they are walking in the Spirit, their desire is to know and follow Jesus, and they are growing in their love for God and one another.

Walking in the Spirit also means denying the flesh, which in this context means all the sinful ways that are characteristic of fallen mankind. The flesh is all that a person is before he is born again. The flesh is at war with the Spirit (Gal. 5:16,17). Scripture lists some of the works of the flesh as being "adultery, fornication, uncleanness, lasciviousness, idolatry, witchcraft, hatred, variance, emulations, wrath, strife, seditions, heresies, envyings, murders, drunkenness, revellings" (Gal. 5:19-21), lying, stealing, bitterness, anger, clamour, evil speaking, and malice (Eph. 4: 25-31). In short, the flesh is self wanting its own way at the expense of others and in opposition to God. The flesh is self on the throne instead of God. One can easily see how vital it is for believers to walk in the Spirit and to deny the fleshly self. And yet, when people experience problems of living, they often attempt to deal with them through fleshly means.

Through encouragement to grow in their walk with the Lord and to depend on Him, believers not only learn to deal with current problems; they will also become better prepared for future trials and challenges they have not yet faced. Rather than getting into the habit of looking to another person to fix their lives or solve their problems, believers will become established in their own walk with the Lord and in drawing upon the resources they already have in Christ. Biblical ministry is for the sake of building up believers in Christ so that they can walk pleasing to the Lord, serving Him, thanking Him, and glorifying Him through good times and bad (Phil. 4:12).

Moving Away from Problem-Centered Counseling

One of Satan's primary ways of working is to overshadow and undermine the real with a deceptively flawed facsimile. Therefore we are calling believers back to the Lord and His Word and back to their new life in Christ, totally without the aid of psychology and totally without the use of counseling manuals, seminars, conferences, workshops, degrees and certificates devised by the biblical counseling movement. And, totally accomplished at the local church level!

Probably the greatest challenge of moving into the personal ministry of mutual care is the usual preoccupation with problems and with sinfully describing and discussing them in detail. The idea of finding help through talking about oneself and about one's problems is firmly embedded in the minds of most Christians. Therefore moving away from problem-centeredness is one of the most difficult tasks in a Christ-centered personal ministry of mutual care. In fact one measure of progress will be that problem-centeredness will fade away and the time will be devoted to spiritual matters. When people become immersed in problems, they often begin to walk by sight instead of by faith. They lose hope. They cannot see God's love in the midst of the trial and thereby they revert to the flesh. They need encouragement regarding Christ's presence, care, involvement, and enabling as they seek to follow Him through difficult circumstances. Drawing their attention back to Christ encourages faith, hope, and love.

The personal ministry of mutual care in the Body of Christ is a spiritual work. It cannot operate according to the flesh, because that will only increase the power of the flesh. Thus there needs to be a 180 degree turnaround from sin-laden counseling conversations to reminding one another what the Bible says about salvation and spiritual growth. The conversations of ministry must revolve around faith and trust in the Lord and His Word—faith that, as believers draw close to God and grow in their faith and love for Him, they will be operating according to God's way regarding their current and future problems. Thus, if problems are discussed, the direction of conversation would be to use these problems for spiritual growth, from the perspective of God's Word without violating Scripture along the way.

Believers who minister to one another do **not** need to use a "Personal Data Inventory" (PDI) because it is problem-centered. (See Chapter 9.) In addition, no other form searching for personal, health, marriage, or family information is necessary, because the **personal ministry of mutual care is not counseling** with all its psychological ramifications. Neither is there a need for note-taking. The Bible and the ministry of Paul never give an example of problem-centered counseling and the accompanying psychological format to justify the use of the PDI or note-taking when ministering to fellow Christians.

Pattern for Personal Soul Care

We live in a fallen, sin-laden world filled with sinners with deceptive hearts. Most people, even many Christians have a light view of sin and deny the fact that depravity touches every aspect of our being. Even after salvation, the old nature retains these sinful tendencies and strives to regain control over the Christian. Therefore the deceptive heart can be extremely active in counseling, particularly the kind of counseling that attempts to reveal a counselee's heart and motivation:

> The heart is deceitful above all things, and desperately wicked: who can know it? I the LORD search the heart, I try the reins, even to give every man according to his ways, and according to the fruit of his doings (Jeremiah 17:9).

It is very easy for the deceptive heart of the old sinful nature to describe their problems in ways that cast blame on circumstances and other people, to speak evil of others, to gossip, to tell biased tales, and to justify self. And, it is very easy for the deceptive heart of the counselor to dig for more. Sin does not overcome or get rid of sin. Instead, sinfulness increases because a pattern of sin has been set up.

An **entirely different pattern** must be followed in a biblical ministry of mutual care. Instead of trying to deal directly with the problem by sinfully discussing all kinds of details, the Bible teaches that believers have been given new life in Christ and that every trial or situation should be seen as an opportunity to grow spiritually—to learn to walk according the new life through the indwelling and empowering Holy Spirit. Therefore, Paul even gloried in even the most trying circumstances:

> Therefore being justified by faith, we have peace with God through our Lord Jesus Christ, by whom also we have access by faith into this grace wherein we stand, and rejoice in hope of the glory of God. And not only so, but we glory in tribulations also: knowing that tribulation wor-

keth patience; And hope maketh not ashamed; because the love of God is shed abroad in our hearts by the Holy Ghost which is given unto us (Rom. 5:1-5).

As Christians use difficulties, daily irritations, insults, long-term trials, and all kinds of problems as reminders to cleave unto the Lord, trust Him, and obey His Word, they will learn to walk according to the Spirit. This is the pattern God provided through Christ: walk according to the spirit (the new life empowered by the Holy Spirit) and put off the old nature (old man, flesh) whenever it appears. This is the pattern for living in Christ and it is the pattern for personal soul care. Those who minister must be learning to walk according to the spirit on a daily basis and during ministry they are to maintain that walk and not slip into conversations stimulated by the sinful nature. But, if they slip, they are to immediately put off the old sinful nature and again put on the new life in Christ. **Those who minister will strive to model the pattern of living by their new life in Christ.**

The one who ministers and the one to whom ministry is given both need to be confident of the fact that the Bible (the Word) trumps the problem-centered (words) format used by both psychological and biblical counselors. Also, the one who ministers and the one to whom ministry is given need to be alert to measure their conversations with biblical standards and not sink into sinful speaking. Sinful conversations are so prevalent in daily living and in counseling that they will be difficult to avoid.

First Things First

The following elements of ministry are brief suggestions that can be used much of the time, but even if they are not used directly, they should be kept in mind. When an individual or couple seeks ministry, a first important task, as an expression of love, is to help individuals refrain from any evil speaking (Eph. 4:31). If a couple is in contention, it is best to minister to each one separately at the beginning, to prevent sinful expressions of deceitful hearts (Jer. 17:9) that are bound to take over. Helping fellow believers realize the presence of Christ and the fact that He knows all about them and desires to work His will in and through them will help move the conversation in the best direction. Praying Psalm 19:14: "Let the words of my mouth, and the meditation of my heart, be acceptable in thy sight, O LORD, my strength, and my redeemer" at the beginning would immediately set a standard for what follows. There are many other verses that should guide the ministry conversations, such as:

Proverbs 18:17: "He that is first in his own cause seemeth just; but his neighbour cometh and searcheth him."

Ephesians 4:29: "Let no corrupt communication proceed out of your mouth, but that which is good to the use of edifying, that it may minister grace unto the hearers."

Ephesians 5:11-12: "And have no fellowship with the unfruitful works of darkness, but rather reprove them. For it is a shame even to speak of those things which are done of them in secret."

Ephesians 6:2-3: "Honour thy father and mother; (which is the first commandment with promise;) That it may be well with thee, and thou mayest live long on the earth."

James 1:26: "If any man among you seem to be religious, and bridleth not his tongue, but deceiveth his own heart, this man's religion is vain."

Whether or not Psalm 19:14 or similar verses are used in personal ministry, they should be kept in mind by the one who ministers mutual care, since individuals in need of help may tend to follow the usual sinful problem-centered obsession with its talebearing and soon need to be brought to a biblical bridling of the tongue for their own spiritual good.

After praying and setting the biblical standard for communicating, it is helpful to review certain basic doctrines of salvation and sanctification. God created mankind in His own image: "in the image of God created he him; male and female created he them" (Gen. 1:27). God created mankind to live in a love relationship with Himself, but sin marred the image and the relationship. However, God in foreknowledge knew this would happen and therefore provided a way to bring mankind back into relationship with Himself: "For God so loved the world, that he gave his only begotten Son, that whosoever believeth in him should not perish, but have everlasting life" (John 3:16).

In response to God's great love, His children are called to "love the Lord thy God with all thy heart, and with all thy soul, and with all thy mind, and with all thy strength: this is the first commandment. And the second is like, namely this, Thou shalt love thy neighbour as thyself. There is none other commandment greater than these" (Mark 12: 30-31). Therefore love for God and others is the essence of the Christian life and of biblical ministry. This kind of love is a giving, self-sacrificing love: "And walk in love, as Christ also hath loved us, and hath given himself for us an offering and a sacrifice to God for a sweetsmelling savour (Eph. 5:2). This is a tall order, but God has made the way through the death and resurrection of Jesus Christ. By dying in the place of sinners, Christ not only paid the penalty of sin but provided new life for believers. From the point of salvation or new birth, the Holy Spirit resides in each believer to guide and empower the new life. As a result, believers are enabled to walk according to the Spirit. At the same time they maintain the ability to choose, and the primary choice is to walk according to the new life or according to the ways of the old self.

It is also needful to spend some time finding out about the person's faith and daily walk with the Lord. Even when Christian service and other evidences of the faith are apparent it is useful to review the essentials of the faith: that all have sinned and come short of the glory of God and that the only remedy is faith in the finished work of Christ dying in the sinner's place and giving new life whereby a believer is enabled to walk according to the Spirit rather than according to the old ways of the flesh. Believers are saved by grace through faith, not by their own works. The Holy Spirit, given at salvation, works from the inside out as Christians trust the Lord and purpose to live according to their new life in Christ. Notice how the pattern of living and ministering according to the new life in Christ moves believers towards spiritual growth and enables them to deal with problems of living without sinful counseling conversations.

Daily Walk

A good follow-up is to explore the current daily expressions of a one's faith (Daily Walk). Since the biblical way through suffering and trials is by walking with the Lord on a daily basis, **a primary goal of personal ministry should be to encourage one another in walking daily with Him**. This daily walk involves thinking, feeling, deciding, and doing in reference to the Lord. It is very easy to drift into walking according to the ways of the fleshly self in thoughts, desires, plans, and purposes. People may even be doing what is moral, but acting according to the life and effort of the flesh rather than according to their new life in Christ.

The goal of a daily walk may be new to some people. Those who are not accustomed to reading Scripture and praying on a consistent daily basis may feel overwhelmed by "one more thing to do." However by beginning with small increments each day, they may discover the joy of a daily walk with Jesus. Daily "lite" can consist of having a Scripture verse on a card nearby or in one's pocket to refer to during the day as a reminder of God's love and presence and reminder to turn to Him in prayer and thanksgiving when temptations, sinful thoughts, or other challenges arise. The daily card can also be useful for memorizing Scripture, so that when one Scripture has been memorized another can take its place until one has a stack of verses that can be reviewed. One can add additional components, such as daily reading one or more chapters from the Bible. It is important for believers to remember the Lord throughout the day and take brief moments to praise, thank, worship, and adore Him. Numerous Scriptures are helpful reminders, such as Psalm 100, which praises the Lord for His goodness to His children.

Since God is love, believers will seek to follow Him in developing their love for God and for one another. A primary Scripture to emphasize early on, particularly when the issue at hand is relational, is 1 Corinthians 13:4-7:

> Charity suffereth long, and is kind; charity envieth not; charity vaunteth not itself, is not puffed up, Doth not behave itself unseemly, seeketh not her own, is not easily provoked, thinketh no evil; Rejoiceth not in iniquity, but rejoiceth in the truth; Beareth all things, believeth all things, hopeth all things, endureth all things.

As believers think about this verse throughout the day, they may notice when they are unloving and take opportunities to confess their sins, be cleansed, and walk again according to the Spirit. As one friend mentioned, walking according to the Spirit is "being 1 John 1:9 up to the nanosecond." By this he means that, whenever he catches himself not walking in love according to the Spirit, he confesses his sin and turns back to walking according to the new life Jesus has given him. Applying 1 Corinthians 1:13:4-7 with 1 John 1:9 provides moment by moment practice in walking daily with the Lord.

Daily "lite" includes some of the basic necessities for nurturing the Spiritual life, but as one grows one will find that "lite" is not enough. As believers mature, they will want the full measure of daily nutrition and will therefore add more time for studying Scripture, praying, and worshipping. They will also find that they want more of the Lord during the day and will therefore add more times during the day of turning aside in prayer and thanksgiving. They will memorize Scripture to fill their minds with ongoing spiritual nutrition and to be ready with wisdom and truth for the needs of the moment. They will want to utilize the spiritual nutrition through the daily exercise of love, obedience, and service.

The Role of Problems

Every problem in life is an opportunity for spiritual growth (Romans 5:1-5; Romans 8:28-29). Believers often pray for God to change the other person, when they, themselves, are in a perfect place to draw close to the Lord, to come to know Him more deeply, and to love Him more completely. Since the way we view problems will influence our course of action, believers need to think seriously about God in relation to every problem of living, not just to seek a solution, but to seek God Himself. In dependence on God and trust in His Word, believers can help shift the attention away from self and problems and towards the Lord Himself, as He creatively works in His children through the challenges and trials of life for His glory and their good.

The world sees problems as impediments to accomplishments, progress, and happiness. The idea is to get through problems and solve them as soon as possible so that one can get on with life. The Bible presents an entirely different perspective on problems of living and even on the most horrendous trials. Therefore, helping fellow believers gain a biblical perspective on their own circumstances and problems of living will help them rightly respond and benefit from whatever trials, afflictions, and problems of living they are experiencing. Problems of living can be like torn up ground in one's life wherein the Lord's Word can be sown and watered. Trials attack faith and test it, and they can be used to strengthen faith and foster spiritual growth (Romans 5:3-5). As problems occur in the lives of His children, God is able to accomplish a far greater feat than we can ever imagine as He uses them to conform His children unto the image of Christ (Romans 8:28-29).

According to His eternal plan and wisdom, God uses mankind's challenges, trials, and sufferings to reveal His glory, to show forth the nature of man, to expose sin, to draw people into relationship with Himself through the Gospel, and to bring forth spiritual growth in His children. Throughout Scripture God used trying circumstances to accomplish His purposes, and He uses problems of living in the lives of believers today. Those in whom Christ dwells can be confident that their own problems are not without some good purpose.

Being grateful to God for how He can turn difficulties into blessings leaves little room for emphasizing a stance of victimhood. Too often counseling encourages a victim role. Such victimization diverts believers away from the cross of Christ. Victimization robs them of gratitude for God's unspeakable gift and thereby robs them of a close walk with Him. Turning Christians into victims weakens their faith and stunts spiritual growth. Every choice to walk according to the Spirit by grace through faith brings spiritual maturity. The choice is up to every believer, whether to be a defined according to the ways of the world with a victimhood stance or to be a biblically defined sinner saved by grace and growing in the likeness of Christ.

Many purposes are fulfilled through trials that work for the good of believers. However, trials in themselves are not necessarily beneficial; it is what God works in the believer through the trials. It is also how the believer responds to God in the midst of those trials. The same trial may afflict two different people, with one turning to God in faith and the other one blaming other people, circumstances, and even God Himself. Obviously one leads towards God and the other away from God. Therefore as believers experience trials we desire to encourage one another to trust God to use them for good.

Christ-Centered Mutual Care

Christ-centered mutual care focuses on Christ because that is the way people are changed into His likeness: "But we all, with open face beholding as in a glass the glory of the Lord, are changed into the same image from glory to glory, even as by the Spirit of the Lord" (2 Cor. 3:18). Because the focus is on Christ and His life in the believer, there is no need to explore a person's past and there is no biblical basis. The Bible includes the past works of God in history, because we are to remember the works of God both individually and corporately. But, regarding the Christian walk, the cross took care of the sins of the past, both sins committed and those committed against oneself. The walk of the believer is to be according to the new life and is therefore present and future oriented. In Philippians 3 Paul gives his religious and personal background, on which he had depended for righteousness before God. But when confronted by

Jesus, he saw his own wretched sinfulness, not only that he had persecuted the church, but that he was sinful to the core. He knew he could not make himself righteous by going back into his past. Therefore he declared: "This one thing I do, forgetting those things which are behind, and reaching forth unto those things which are before, I press toward the mark for the prize of the high calling of God in Christ Jesus" (Phil. 3:13-14). This does not mean an inability to recall the past; it means that the past now has a different significance. Biblically speaking, attempting to fix the past is purely a fleshly activity that wars against the Spirit, unless there is need for confession, repentance, and restitution.

A person need not be trapped in negative patterns of behavior established in the early years of life, for the Bible offers a new way of life. Put off the old man; put on the new. Jesus said to Nicodemus, "Ye must be born again" (John 3:7), and He said elsewhere that new wine could not be put into old wineskins (Matt. 9:17). Jesus offers new life and new beginnings. One who is born again has the spiritual capacity to overcome old ways and develop new ones through the action of the Holy Spirit, the fruit of the Spirit, and the sanctification of the believer. One wonders why so many have given up the hope of Christianity for the hopelessness of past determinism.

Christ dealt with every believer's past at the cross when he died for their sins. When believers identify with Christ's death and resurrection they are free from the past of the flesh as well as the power of the flesh. They have a new life in Christ and are to live according to that new life. **Attempts to heal the hurts of the past are futile,** because one is not to heal that which is to be counted dead and buried (Romans 6:3-11). Such sinful attempts give power to the flesh and will result in fleshly living in place of walking according to the Spirit. Christ-centered mutual care will encourage and help a seeker **leave the past at the foot of the cross** and to "press toward the mark for the prize of the high calling of God in Christ Jesus" (Phil. 3:14).

Mutual care givers do not need to talk about a fellow believer's mother or father, but will encourage the direction away from blaming parents and past circumstances and towards the goal of growing spiritually into the likeness of Christ. Jesus, the Word of God, and the work of the Holy Spirit will be the emphasis. After all, every true believer has been born again and has a new Father, a new life, a new family, and an indwelling Holy Spirit.

Ministering Christ to One Another

Christ-centered mutual care is reflecting and expressing the Life of Christ. How one does that is truly a mystery. It is the mystery of "Christ in you, the hope of glory" (Col. 1:27). It is a spiritual activity of Jesus Christ Himself through the Holy Spirit and through members of His Body. Therefore, mutual care is not a methodology but Jesus working through believers as they come together. Christ must be preeminent in the thinking, speaking, and doing among members of His Body. If He is at the center, true ministry happens. Life comes forth and people are blessed as they respond in faith.

Jesus ministered differently to each person, because He knew each one's need. He still does, and those who minister to one another need to follow Him in being sensitive to what is needful for each person. Only the Lord knows how much of mercy and truth to apply. Sometimes a suffering soul needs a gentle word emphasizing the mercy, grace, and nurture of the Lord—His love and caring. At other times a fellow believer would be motivated better by a direct word of truth, emphasizing God's justice and serving as an admonition. Paul gives a brief example of ministering differently to each individual: "Now we exhort you, brethren, warn them that are unruly, comfort the feebleminded, support the weak, be patient toward all men" (1 Thes. 5:14). At each moment, the ministering helper must listen with both the physical ear and the spiritual ear. The Lord is faithful to lead as He is acknowledged in the heart every moment throughout any time of ministry (Proverbs 3:5-6).

Love is the essence of the Gospel and of the new life in Christ. Therefore love must be foremost in mutual care. Jesus said we are to love one another as He has loved us. That means to love one another sacrificially (John 15:12,13), without regard for a person's wealth or station in life (Romans 12:16; James 2:1-24). Paul reminds believers to "be kindly affectioned one to another with brotherly love; in honour preferring one another" (Rom. 12:10). That means putting the other person first. Love is something freely given, without charge.

God has demonstrated His love through His Word and through all that Christ did to secure our salvation and to give us new life. Through His Word, God has also revealed the inner man of all people born upon this earth. He has revealed their heart, their spiritual condition, and the nature of their soul. He also knows the problems people are facing and is able to give wisdom and insight directly to the person in need without the helper needing to know the details. Moreover He has provided the only means of real change—from spiritual death to new life. He has provided the only means of nourishing that new life: through His Word, His Spirit, and His Body. The new life must have spiritual food and cannot be nourished through the wisdom or ways of the world. Therefore the Word of God is to be ministered by the indwelling Holy Spirit and by the life of Christ ministered to one another in the Body of Christ.

The goal of biblical ministry is to encourage people to draw closer to God—to look to Him and to love, serve, and obey Him. While drawing people closer to God may not change their circumstances, it will accomplish far more on the inside as they learn to walk according to the spirit. As people are encouraged to draw close to God, they will find His perspective as well as His provision and His will as well as His willingness to help. Every believer can be a source of encouragement.

The Word of God is a vast resource. It provides all the information one needs for being saved and sanctified, for knowing God's love, for loving God and one another, for living the new life in Christ, for denying self, and for spiritual warfare. The Word of God is powerful and the doctrines of Scripture are dynamic. There's more power, wisdom, healing, and help in any truth from Scripture than from all the psychological theories and therapies conceived by those who devised or utilize the nearly 500 different systems of psychotherapy with their thousands of techniques.

Believers Called and Empowered

Believers are called and empowered to serve in the Body of Christ. The Lord will enable them to serve as they are constant in prayer, knowledgeable of the Word, and marked with the humility of a servant's heart as they are ready to serve without having to be in a superior position or to have a title of superiority.

For believers to minister in the direction of growing spiritually and walking according to the Spirit, they themselves must be established in the faith, trusting and obeying Christ, and seeking to serve Him daily in whatever they are doing. As believers are established and equipped in their own walk with Christ and as they are taught, reminded, encouraged, and exhorted along the way, they will be able to teach, remind, encourage, exhort one another to walk according to the new life purchased by Christ on the cross. However, they need to be mindful of the fact that they must keep themselves and their ministry in the Lord from slipping into the old ways of the flesh. The arch enemy of souls does all he can to disrupt and dissuade believers from walking according to the Spirit and ministering to one another according to the Spirit.

When ministry is one-to-one, we advise men should minister to men and women to women. Not only does this arrangement avoid sexual temptation; it also avoids having a woman usurp authority over a man. In addition, only a man knows what it is to follow Christ in his manhood and in the roles of leadership he has been given in the family and church. Only a woman knows what it is to follow Christ in her womanhood and in the role requiring submission to a spouse. Scripture has numerous examples of men ministering to men, and Scripture calls the older women to minister to the younger ones.

> The aged women likewise, that they be in behaviour as becometh holiness, not false accusers, not given to much wine, teachers of good things; that they may teach the young women to be sober, to love their husbands, to love their children, to be discreet, chaste, keepers at home, good, obedient to their own husbands, that the word of God be not blasphemed (Titus 2:3-5).

Notice how the person's life teaches as well as the words. Throughout Scripture we see such examples of how a great deal of teaching and ministry in the Body of Christ is by example—by simply living the new life rather than the old.

Those who minister by the Word and the Spirit will be challenged in their own walk with the Lord, for they, themselves, must not only model walking according to the Spirit, but they must receive correction from the Lord along the way. They must know what the Bible says about how people are to communicate with each other and follow its admonitions, prohibitions, and restrictions, because every word, every sentence, and every emotion expressed during ministry that does not conform to Scripture will fail to model the new life in Christ. Any personal ministry that allows or even encourages violations of Scripture regarding the tongue will fail at nurturing the spiritual walk. In contrast, taming the tongue and bringing thoughts and words to the obedience of Christ will serve to model the Christian walk.

Those who are called to minister the life of Christ must themselves practice walking according to the Spirit in their own daily lives in relation to other people and circumstances. This is a high calling, but in reality it is the calling of every believer to walk according to the Spirit rather than the flesh. As such, walking according to the Spirit is essential in personal care ministry. At the same time, those who consciously determine to walk according to the Spirit will find that it is not easy. In fact, without the very presence and power of the Lord, it is impossible. It requires much dying to self as one notices numerous ways in which the old nature takes over. There will be a continual turning oneself over to the Lord for His life to take over. Believers are called and equipped to be ambassadors of Christ—to be a reflection of Him. Therefore believers who minister in any capacity must strive to be an example of biblical living in the home, in the church, at work, and in society.

When believers truly desire to please God in their attitude, thoughts, words, and actions, they will give attention to what the Word says and the Holy Spirit will be faithful to teach, convict, and enable:

> All scripture is given by inspiration of God, and is profitable for doctrine, for reproof, for correction, for instruction in righteousness: That the man of God may be perfect, throughly furnished unto all good works." (2 Tim. 3:16-17.).

As believers minister to one another those who minister carry the burden of responsibility for their own words and also for the direction of the conversation so that it does not deteriorate into gossiping, complaining about other people, blaming, or playing the victim. Instead of probing and prying for more details, those who minister should be leading the conversation in the direction of edification—that believers will learn to grow spiritually through all challenges, trials, difficulties, and problems and that whatever is said or done will glorify God. As believers follow this pattern of walking according to their new life in Christ in varying circumstances, they will be genuinely and consistently walking with the Lord in their thoughts, words, attitudes, and actions in such a way as to encourage other believers to follow the same biblical pattern of walking according to the Spirit rather than the old nature.

Ministry among believers should be constant and ongoing, which will result in souls beset with problems seeking the Lord through His Spirit, Word, and Body rather than turning to counseling. What a privilege to be included in the mighty, miraculous work of God in one another's lives. All believers have opportunities to minister to fellow believers to encourage them along the way.

If you are one who is experiencing problems of living and looking for assistance, find someone in your local church who can minister to you. Find someone who is mature in the faith and is walking with God the way you desire to walk. Ask that person to come alongside, minister the Life of Christ, speak forth the truth of God, encourage you in your walk with the Lord, and earnestly pray.

If you are a Christian, know essential biblical doctrines, are walking according to your new life in Christ and growing in the Lord, you already have what it takes to minister the Life of Christ to a fellow believer. You have a living God, the source of all life and healing. You have His living, enduring, abiding Word (1 Peter 1:23-25), which ministers truth to the mind, direction and encouragement to the will, and grace for the emotions. The personal ministry of mutual care is not a position of expertise (one-up-man-ship) but one of side-by-side seeking the Lord. It does not lead believers into the downward spiral of problems, but rather upward to the Life of Christ and the Word of God through the work of the Holy Spirit.

Can you think of anything more worthwhile than to serve God in your own family, in the Body of Christ, and in the world? Every person in whom the Holy Spirit lives is enabled to serve and can say with Paul, "I can do all things through Christ which strengtheneth me" (Phil. 4:13)? Take courage! God will indeed work His own good pleasure in and through His children.

We repeat from the beginning of this chapter: In **most cases** of personal ministry, it is both not possible and not necessary to know for sure whether or not such disorders or challenges are the result of an objective biological illness. And, a first priority for personal ministry is to **follow biblical guidelines for speaking and listening to one another**. Once the problem-centered sinful counseling is avoided, ministry can proceed biblically with anyone who needs help and desires to grow spiritually—to walk according to the new life in Christ.

Person to Person Ministry[1]

Person-to-person ministry is not only for those who seek such help. It is for every believer as various needs arise. This kind of ministry thrives in true Christian fellowship as believers encourage one another in following Christ, and it can occur anywhere from within the family to out in the community, as believers happen to see each other. However, it can also be a very purposeful ministry of reaching out to those in need, such as those suffering the trials of physical illness, those who are infirmed and elderly, families that have lost loved ones, young parents who could use a little encouragement and practical help, those who have not yet been incorporated into the life of the church, those who could benefit from personal discipleship, and others who may simply need a ride to church. These are the kinds of person-to-person ministry that are hidden and not broadcast abroad. They do not have the prestige of "counselor," but they are exceedingly pleasing to God. Such person-to-person ministry is the true ministry of mutual care. In fact, if Christians were to purposefully involve themselves in this mutual care there would be few who would seek problem-centered counseling help.

Person-to-person ministry is shared among the body of believers so that the dependency is on Christ in the context of His Body. It should follow the natural function of the body as described in Romans 12 where believers share the joys and sorrows of life with one another. It does not function as an entity unto itself, as so much of the biblical counseling movement does, confined to counseling offices and problem-centered conversations. While the one who ministers can meet someone in a church office, there is no such limitation in person-to-person ministry. The biblical helper may minister to individuals, couples, and families in homes, as well as in a great variety of other places. Furthermore, the relationship of love and care goes beyond conversation when practical assistance is needed, just as James 2:15-16 says:

> If a brother or sister be naked, and destitute of daily food, And one of you say unto them, Depart in peace, be ye warmed and filled; notwithstanding ye give them not those things which are needful to the body; what doth it profit?

And, of course all of this can be shared within the fellowship of believers.

When believers are walking according to the Spirit and seeking to serve the Lord they will find opportunities to minister. In fact, they may find more opportunities than they can fulfill and that is where they can encourage fellow believers to come alongside and join them in mutual care. Churches may develop programs in their attempt to meet various needs, but so often the programs become ends in themselves and the normal spiritual function of Christ's Body becomes replaced by programs. Some form of organization may be necessary to inform believers of needs in the fellowship, such as when there is illness and a family needs meals or when fellow believers are in need of visitation or assistance. On the other hand individual believers often know of needs and may seek the Lord as to whether or how they might minister. Much of this should happen naturally as believers fellowship together and grow in their love for one another and as pastors and leaders teach them about mutual care according to the Word.

As believers move away from talking about problems towards giving attention to Christ and growing into His likeness, there will be evidence of spiritual growth. There will be more of Jesus and less of self. There will be greater love for God and others. Believers will be motivated to walk according to the Spirit rather than the flesh and have an earnest desire to please God. They will grow in humility with a keen understanding of the depravity of their own flesh, which is to be put off and counted dead. As believers become more and more occupied with Christ, they will bear more fruit of the Spirit. Then, instead of needing ministry, they will be able to minister to others.

Ever since the Day of Pentecost there have been believers who have turned to the Lord during trials, and there are still many believers who turn to the Lord and spiritually mature through their suffering. These are living epistles of the work of Christ during difficult circumstances. Throughout the centuries God has used ordinary believers to minister His life through the preaching of the Gospel to unbelievers. He also used ordinary believers to minister His Word and His life to fellow believers long before the intrusion of psychological theories and therapies into the church and long before the contemporary biblical counseling movement. We rejoice that even now such Christ-centered ministry continues quietly as needs arise among believers. These are not the people who would be noticed by the world. They are the saints who are seen by the Lord Himself as they labor quietly behind the scenes to minister the life of Christ to one another.

May more believers find their freedom in Christ to step out in faith to minister His Word and His Life for salvation of the lost and for the edification of fellow saints who are suffering from problems of living. May they do so by depending on God, His Word, and His ongoing work in each believer.

Mutual Care Resources:

The following books amplify the means of ministering mutual care in the Body of Christ. These, as well as other Bobgan books, may be purchased both as ebooks and paperback books at Amazon.com. They are also available as free pdf ebooks **for a limited period of time** on the following website: www.pamweb.org.

Competent to Minister: The Biblical Care of Souls

Answers such questions as:

- What can believers do to help individuals suffering from problems of living?
- What should churches do for suffering souls?
- What did the church do for almost 2000 years without psychological counseling?
- What did the church do without the biblical counseling movement which began about 25 years ago?

This book calls Christians back to the Bible and to the biblically ordained ministries and mutual care in the Body of Christ that have effectively cared for souls for almost 2000 years.

Christ-Centered Ministry versus Problem-Centered Counseling

The purpose of this book is to reveal the origins and faults of problem-centered counseling, to describe Christ-centered ministry and how it differs from problem-centered counseling, and to encourage local congregations to minister biblically without the influence of the psychological or biblical counseling movements.

Person to Person Ministry: Soul Care in the Body of Christ

Person to Person Ministry: Soul Care in the Body of Christ is about a Christ-centered approach to nurture the spiritual life of believers and to equip them to fight the good fight of faith and thereby confront problems of living through exercising faith in Christ and the Word. This book also reveals the innate sinfulness of problem-centered counseling, shows how problem-centered counseling leads Christians into feeding the flesh and quenching the Spirit, and gives reasons why Christians must abandon the problem-centered approach.

Stop Counseling! Start Ministering!

Stop Counseling! Start Ministering! tells why Christians should be opposed to counseling, literally Stop Counseling! and Start Ministering! Reasons are revealed why counseling, because it is problem-centered, inevitably involves sinful conversations. Central to ministering is helping individuals in need to overcome their fixation on their problems and encouraging them to become Christ-centered on a daily basis. This book provides ways of equipping those in need with the truths of Scripture and encouraging them to live the daily life that will be honoring to the Lord and beneficial for meeting life's problems without sinfully talking about them.

May God bless you as you seek to participate with Him in mutual care in the body of Christ.

End Notes

Chapter 1 The Rise and Use of the Medical Model of Mental Illness

1   Exceptions would be to known illnesses that may affect the thinking and behavior of an individual.

2   Lawrence LeShan, *Association for Humanistic Psychology*, October, 1984, p. 4.

3   E. Fuller Torrey. *The Death of Psychiatry*. Radnor, PA: Chilton Book Company, 1974, p. 8.

4   *Ibid*, p. 7.

5   Robert C. Fuller. *Mesmerism and the American Cure of Souls*. Philadelphia: University of Pennsylvania Press, 1982, p. 1.

6   Thomas Szasz. *The Myth of Psychotherapy*. Garden City: Doubleday/Anchor Press, 1978, p. 43.

7   E. M. Thornton, *The Freudian Fallacy* (Garden City: The Dial Press, Doubleday and Company, 1984), p. ix.

8   Szasz, *op. cit.*, p. 3.

9   *Ibid.*, p. 6.

10 *Ibid.*, pp. 104-105.

11 Ellen Herman. *The Romance of American Psychology*. Berkeley: University of California Press, 1996, p.3.

12 *Ibid.*, p. 5.

13 Jonathan Engel. *American Therapy: The Rise of Psychotherapy in the United States*. New York: Gotham Books, 2008, dust jacket.

14 *Ibid.*, p. XIV.

15 Herman, *op. cit.*, p. 275.

16 *Ibid.*, p. 311.

17 Phone call to the United States Conference of Catholic Bishops, 202-541-3200.

18 Janice Peck. *The Age of Oprah: Cultural Icon for the Neoliberal Era*. Boulder. CO: Paradigm Publishers, 2008, p. 18.

19 Steven Stosny, "Case Studies," *Psychotherapy Networker*, Vol. 33, No. 2, p. 65.

20 Eva Moskowitz. *In Therapy We Trust: America's Obsession with Self-Fulfillment*. Baltimore: The Johns Hopkins University Press, 2001, p. 8.

21 Frank Furedi. *Therapy Culture*. New York: Routledge, 2004, p. 18.

22 Sudhir Kakar, "Western Science, Eastern Minds," *The Wilson Quarterly*, Vol. XV, No. 1, p. 114.

23 David Brooks, "Harmony and the Dream," *The New York Times*, 8/11/2008.

24 Skye Stephenson. *Understanding Spanish-Speaking South Americans: Bridging Hemispheres*. Yarmouth, ME: Intercultural Press, Inc., p. 47.

25 *Ibid.*, pp. 60-61.

26 G. Hofstede and G.J. Hofstede. *Cultures and Organizations: Software of the Mind*. New York: McGraw Hill, 2005, p. 76.

27 *Ibid.*, p. 98.

28 John T. McNeill. A *History of the Cure of Souls*. New York: Harper and Row, 1951, p. vii.

29 Szasz, *op. cit.*, p. xviii.

30 *Ibid.*, p. xxiv.

31 *Ibid.*, p. 26.

32 *Ibid.*, p. 138.

33 *Ibid.*, p. 27.

34 Torrey, *op. cit.*, p. 21.

35 Martin and Deidre Bobgan. *PsychoHeresy*, Revised & Expanded. Santa Barbara, CA: EastGate Publishers, 2012.

Chapter 2 The *DSM* and Mental Illness

1   E. Fuller Torrey. *The Death of Psychiatry*. Radnor, PA: Chilton Book Company, 1974. Jacket cover.

2   "*DSM-5*: Frequently Asked Questions: What is DSM and why it is important?" American Psychiatric Association, https://www.psychiatry.org.

3   "4 Controversial Mental Disorders," Paula Derrow, *Berkeley Wellness Letter*, 9/10/2015,www.berkeleywellness,com.

4   "*DSM-5*: Psychiatrists' 'Bible' Finally Unveiled," *Huffington Post*, 05/16/2013, www.huffingtonpost.com.

5   Torrey, *The Death of Psychiatry*, *op. cit.*, p. 38.

6   Schildkrout. *Masquerading Symptoms, op. cit.*, p. 217.

7   Mary Sykes Wylie and Richard Simon, "Discoveries from the Black Box," *Psychotherapy Networker*, Vol. 26, No. 5, p. 26.

8   Christof Koch, quoted in *The New York Times*, Oct. 14, 2018, www.nytimes.com.

9   *Psychology Today*, Vol. 35, No. 3, p. 17.

10 Stephen Smith quoted by Bruce Goldman, "New imaging method developed at Stanford reveals stunning details of brain connections," *Stanford Medicine News Center*, 11/17/2010. https://med.stanford.edu/news/all-news/2010/11/new-imaging-method-developed-at-stanford-reveals-stunning-details-of-brain-connections.html.

11 David Cloud, "The Human Brain," *Friday Church Notes*, 10/19/2018, wayoflife.org.

12 Torrey, *The Death of Psychiatry*, *op. cit.*, p. 39.

13 https://www.smithsonianmag.com/smart-news/there-are-372-trillion-cells-in-your-body-4941473/.

14 Michael Chase, "The Matriculating Brain," *Psychology Today,* June 1973, p. 82.

15 Emeran Mayer. *The Mind-Gut Connection*. New York: HarperCollins Publishers, 2016, p. 14.

16 *Ibid.*, p. 16.

17 *Ibid.*, pp. 95-96.

18 Marilia Caraotti et al, "The Gut-brain axis: Interactions between enteric microbiota, central and enteric nervous systems," *Annals of Gastroenterology*, Vol. 28, No. 2, April-June, 2015, pp. 203-209, https://www.ncbi.nlm.nih.gov/pmc/articles/PMC4367209/.

19 Jane A. Foster and Karen-Anne McVey Neufeld, "Gut-brain axis: how the microbiome influences anxiety and depression," *Trends in Neuroscience*, May 2013, Vol. 36, No. 5,pp 305-312, http://neuroscienceresearch.wustl.edu/userfiles/file/Gut_brain%20axis%20How%20the%20microbiome%20influences%20anxiety%20and%20depression_Tran%20%20%20.pdf.

20 Robert L. Spitzer, "Foreword." Allan V, Horwitz and Jerome C. Wakefield. *The Loss of Sadness: How Psychiatry Transformed Normal Sorrow into Depressive Disorder*. New York: Oxford University Press, 2007, p. vii.

21 Torrey, *The Death of Psychiatry, op. cit.*, p. 38.

22 *Ibid.*, p. 40.

23 "Diagnostic and Statistical manual of Mental Disorders," https://en.wikipedia.org/wiki/Diagnostic_and_Statistical_Manual_of_Mental_Disorders, 10/24/2016.

24 J. Katz. In *U. S. v. Torniero*, 570 F. Supp. 721. D.C. Conn, 1983; quoted in R. Slovenko, "The Meaning of Mental Illness in Criminal Responsibility," *Journal of Legal Medicine*, Vol. 5, March 1984 1-61.

25 Jonas Robitscher. *The Powers of Psychiatry*. Boston: Houghton Mifflin Company, 1980, p. 166.

26 "AAPL and DSM-111, *"Newsletter of the American Academy of Psychiatry and the Law,* Summer 1976, p. 11.

27 "DSM-5 And Caffeine Intoxication: Could Coffee-Drinking Brew a Mental Disorder?" *Huffington Post,* 5/29/2013, www.huffingtonpost.com.

28 "Not All Pedophiles Have Mental Disorder, American Psychiatric Association Says in New DSM," *Huffington Post,* 11/1/2013, www.huffingtonpost.com.

29 Alfred Freedman, Harold Kaplan, and Benjamin Sadock. *Modern Synopsis of Comprehensive Textbook of Psychiatry,* 2nd Ed. Baltimore: Williams & Wilkins, 1976, p. 407.

30 Margaret A. Hagen. *Whores of the Court*. New York: Regan Books/HarperCollins Publishers, 1997, p. 77.

31 *Ibid.*, p. 250.

32 Irwin Savodnik, "Psychiatry's Sick Compulsion: Turning Weaknesses into Diseases," *Los Angeles Times*, Jan. 1, 2006.

33 Sharon Begley, "DSM-5: Psychiatrists' Bible' Finally Unveiled," *Huffington Post*, http://www.huffingtonpost.com/2013/05/17/dsm-5-unveiled-changes-disorders-_n_3290212.html.

34 Savodnik, *op. cit.*

35 Paul Genova, "Dump the *DSM*!" *Psychiatric Times*, Vol. XX, Issue 4.

36 "Pandora's box," www.google.com.

Chapter 3 Misdiagnosis and Maltreatment

1 Kimball Atwood, "Bacteria, Ulcers, and Ostracism?: H. Pylori and the Making of a Myth," *Skeptical Inquirer*, Vol. 28, No. 6.

2 Sidney Walker III. *A Dose of Sanity: Mind, Medicine, and Misdiagnosis*. New York: John Wiley & Sons, Inc., 1996, back cover.

3 Sydney Walker III, "Blood Sugar and Emotional Storms: Sugar Doctors Push Hypoglycemia." *Psychology Today*, July 1975, p. 74.

4 Allen Bergin, "Psychotherapy Can Be Dangerous." *Psychology Today*, Nov. 1975, p. 96.

5 I. S. Cooper. *The Victim Is Always the Same*. New York: Harper and Row, 1973.

6 Ronald P. Lesser and Stanley Fahn, "Dystonia: A Disorder Often Misdiagnosed as a Conversion Reaction." *American Journal of Psychiatry*, Vol. 135, No. 3, March 1978, p. 350.

7 Elizabeth Cohen, "'Widespread and Dangerous,' Facing Medical uncertainty, some doctors tell patients it's all in their heads...," CNN, 12/24/2018, https://www.keyt.com/health/missed-diagnosis-of-poliolike-disease-concerns-parents/949288755.

8 *Ibid.*

9 Barbara Schildkrout. *Unmasking Psychological Symptoms: How Therapists Can Learn to Recognize the Psychological Presentation of Medical Disorders*. Hoboken, NJ: John Wiley & Sons, Inc., 2011.

10 Barbara Schildkrout. *Masquerading Symptoms: Uncovering Physical Illnesses That Present as Psychological Problems*. Hoboken, NJ: John Wiley & Sons, Inc., 2014 (Kindle Edition).

11 E. K. Koranyi (1979), "Morbidity and rate of undiagnosed physical illnesses in a psychiatric clinic population." *Archives of General Psychiatry*, 36(4), 414.

12 Schildkrout. *Masquerading Symptoms*, *op. cit.*, p. xi.

13 *Ibid.*, pp. 15ff.

14 Sumant Khanna, et al, "Viral Antibodies in Blood in Obsessive Compulsive Disorder," *Indian Journal of Psychiatry*, 1997, Vol. 39, No. 3, pp. 190-195, https://www.ncbi.nlm.nih.gov/pmc/articles/PMC2967113/pdf/IJPsy-39-190.pdf.

15 Jeff Sxymanski, Harvard Medical School blog posted 2/27/2012, http://www.health.harvard.edu/blog/can-an-infection-suddenly-cause-ocd-201202274417.

16 *Ibid.*

17 Thomas Szasz, "Nobody Should Decide Who Goes to the Mental Hospital," *Co-Evolution Quarterly*, Summer 1978, p. 60.

18 O. Hobart Mowrer. *The Crisis in Psychiatry and Religion*. Princeton: Van Nostrand Co., Inc., 1961, p. 60.

Chapter 4   The Medical Model of Mental Illness

1 Robert M. Johnson. *A Logic Book*, 2nd Ed. Belmont, CA: Wadsworth Publishing Company, 1992, p. 256.

2 *Ibid.*, p. 258,

3 Thomas Szasz. *The Myth of Psychotherapy*. Garden City: Doubleday/Anchor Press, 1978,pp. 182-183.

4 *Ibid.*, p. 7.

5 Ronald Leifer, *In the Name of Mental Health*. New York: Science House, 1969, pp. 36-37.

6 *Ibid.*, p. 38.

7 E. Fuller Torrey, *The Death of Psychiatry*. Radnor: Chilton Book Company, 1974, p. 24.

8 Martin and Deidre Bobgan. *PsychoHeresy*, Revised and Expanded. Santa Barbara, CA, 2012, Chapter 7.

9 *Ibid.*, Chapter 6.

10 http://www.cdc.gov/mentalhealthsurveillance/fact_sheet.html.

11 http//www.nami.org/template.cfm?section=about_mental_illness.

12 Thomas R. Insel, "Atonement," www.psychiatrictimes.com.

13 http://www.hms.harvard.edu/dms/bbs/fac/mccarroll.php.

14 Jonas Robitscher. *The Powers of Psychiatry*. Boston: Houghton Mifflin Company, 1980, p. 155.

15 Russ Pulliam, "Alcoholism: Sin or Sickness?" *Christianity Today,* 18 September 1981, p. 23.

16 "UCSB Professor Says Alcoholism Not Disease," *Santa Barbara News Press,* 6/10/1984, p. D-3.

17 Pulliam, *op. cit.,* pp. 23-24.

18 Bruce J. Ennis and Thomas R. Litwack, "Psychiatry and the Presumption of Expertise," *California Law Review,* May 1974, p. 741.

19 Ann Landers, *Santa Barbara-News Press,* 3 April 1980, p. B-12.

Chapter 5   Disease, Diagnosis, and Prognosis

1 Thomas Szasz. *The Myth of Psychotherapy*. Garden City: Doubleday/Anchor Press, 1978, p. 25.

2 *Ibid.*, p. 11.

3 Lou Marinoff. *Plato, Not Prozac! Applying External Wisdom to Everyday Problems.* New York: Harper Collins, 1990.

4 Brandon a. Gaudiano, "Examining Philosophical Counseling…Old Wine in New Bottles? Review of the Book *Plato, Not Prozac!*," *The Scientific Review of Mental Health Practice*, Vol. 1, No. 1, p. 82.

5 Jonas Robitscher. *The Powers of Psychiatry.* Boston, MA: Houghton Mifflin Company, 1980, p. 150.

6 Leonard Kurland, "A New Wrinkle in a Colossal Rip-Off," *Los Angeles Times*, 5 September 1980, Part 11, p. 7.

7 *Ibid.,* p. 7.

8 Robitscher, *op. cit.,* p. 161.

9 Mary Stewart Van Leeuwen, "A Christian Examination of Applied Behaviorism," *Journal of the American Scientific Affiliation,* September 1979, pp. 136-137.

10 Jonas Robitscher, *op. cit.,* p. 166.

11 Irwin Savodnik, "Psychiatry's Sick Compulsion: Turning Weaknesses into Diseases," *Los Angeles Times,* Jan. 1, 2006.

12 George Albee, "The Answer Is Prevention," *Psychology Today,* February 1985, p. 61.

13 Walter Reich, "The Force of Diagnosis," *Harper's,* May 1980, p. 24.

14 Martin and Deidre Bobgan. *The Psychological Way/The Spiritual Way.* Minneapolis: Bethany House Publishers, 1979, p. 60.

15 Hugh Drummond, "Dr. D. Is Mad As Hell," *Mother Jones,* December 1979, p. 52.

16 Bobgan, *The Psychological Way/The Spiritual Way, op. cit.,* pp. 61-62.

17 Herb Kutchins and Stuart A. Kirk. *Making Us Crazy.* New York: The Free Press, 1997, p. 53.

18 David Faust and Jay Ziskin, "The Expert Witness in Psychology and Psychiatry," *Science*, Vol. 241, 1 July 1988, p. 32.

19 Albee, *op. cit.,* p. 60.

20 David L. Rosenhan, "On Being Sane in Insane Places," *Science,* January 1973, p. 252.

21 Thomas Szasz. *The Manufacture of Madness.* New York: Harper & Row, Publishers, 1970, p. 35.

22 Christopher Lasch. *Haven in a Heartless World.* New York: Basic Books, Inc., 1977, p. 186.

23 Hillel J. Einhorn and Robin M. Hogarth, "Confidence in Judgment: Persistence of the Illusion of Validity," *Psychological Review,* Vol. 85, No. 5, 1978, p. 395.

24 Bobgan, *The Psychological Way/The Spiritual Way, op. cit.,* p. 46.

25 Robitscher, *op. cit.,* p. 196.

26 Ronald Schiensky quoted by Chet Holcombe, "Mental Health Fund Shift Seen," *Santa Barbara News Press,* 3 January 1980, p. C-8.

27 American Psychiatric Association, Amicus Curiae Brief, Tarasoff v. Regents of University of California, 551 P 2d 334 (Cal, 1976).

28 Jim Mann, "Psychiatry's Role in Court Challenged," *Los Angeles Times, 9* November 1980, Part 1, p. 20.

29 Larry Stammer, "Two Professionals Urge Ban on Psychiatric Testimony," *Los Angeles Times,* 4 December 198 1, Part 1, pp. 3, 8.

30 "Idaho Eliminates Insanity Defense," *Santa Barbara News Press,* 3 April 1982, p. A-6.

31 Thomas Szasz, "Nobody Should Decide Who Goes to the Mental Hospital," *Co-Evolution Quarterly,* Summer 1978, p. 65.

32 Harold Mavritte quoted by John Hurst, "State Mental Health Law," *Los Angeles Times,* 16 June 1980, Part 11, p. 8.

33 Lee Coleman quoted by Howard Kissel, "Putting Psychiatry on the Witness Stand," *Women's Wear Daily,* 10 July 1984, p. 18.

34 Janet Ratloff, "Judging Science," *Science News*, Vol. 173, p. 44.

Chapter 6 The Labeling Game

1 Jonas Robitscher. *The Powers of Psychiatry.* Boston: Houghton Mifflin Company, 1980, p. 151.

2 E. Fuller Torrey. *The Death of Psychiatry.* Radnor: Chilton Book Company, 1974, p. 64.

3 Hugh Drummond, "Dr. D. Is Mad as Hell," *Mother Jones,* December 1979, p. 56.

4 0. R. Gursslin, R. G. Hunt, and J. L. Roach, "Social Class and the Mental Health Movement," *Mental Health of the Poor,* F Riessman, **J.** Cohen, and A. Pearl, eds. New York: The Free Press, 1964, p. 63.

5 Ethan Watters. *Crazy Like Us*. New York: Free Press, 2010, jacket cover.

6 "The Children of Pavlov," *Time,* 23 June 1980, p. 65.

7 Christopher Lasch. *Haven in a Heartless World.* New York: Basic Books, Inc., p. 189.

8 Walter Reich, "The Force of Diagnosis," *Harpers,* May 1980, p. 29.

9 "'Labeling' Causes Observers to See Commonplace Behavior as Neurotic," *Brain/ Mind Bulletin,* 17 March 1980, p. 2.

10 Eric Lewin Altschuler, Ansar Haroun, Bing Ho and Amy Weimer, "Did Samson Have Antisocial Personality Disorder?" *Archives of General Psychiatry*, Vol. 58, Feb., 2001, p. 202.

11 Alison Motlunk,"Seized by God," *The New Scientist,* Vol. 172, No. 2317, p. 20.

12 Drummond, *op. cit.,* p. 56.

13 Reich, *op. cit.,* p. 32.

14 *Ibid.,* pp. 29, 32.

Chapter 7 Mental Illness and Irresponsibility

1   Barbara Brown. *Supermind*. New York: Harper & Row, Publishers, 1980, p. 6..

2   Arthur Custance. *The Mysterious Matter of Mind*. Grand Rapids: Zondervan Publishing House, 1980, p. 9.

3   Shervert Frazier quoted by Lois Timnick, "Psychiatry's Focus Turns to Biology," *Los Angeles Times,* 21 July 1980, part 1, p. 20.

4   Jonas Robitscher. *The Powers of Psychiatry*. Boston: Houghton Mifflin Company, 1980, p. 9.

5   Henry Fairlie. *The Seven Deadly Sins Today.* Washington: New Republic Books, 1978, p. 58.

6   E. Fuller Torrey. *The Death of Psychiatry*. Radnor, PA: Chilton Book Company, 1974., p. 91.

7   *Ibid.*, p. 93.

8   Ibid., p. 182.

9   *Ibid.*, p. 96.

10 *Ibid.*, pp. 43-44.

11 "Ethan Couch" Wikipedia, https://en.wikipedia.org/wiki/Ethan_Couch, 11-28-2018.

12 Thomas Szasz quoted by David Einstein, "Results of Sanity Trials Show Weakness in System," *Santa Barbara News Press,* 26 February 1981, p. B-4.

13 Nils Bolduan, "Helpless Souls Who Wander City Streets," *Santa Barbara News Press,* 12 April 1981, p. A-14.

14 Rousas Rushdoony, "The Chalcedon Report," *Chalcedon,* January 1981, p. 1.

15 Rousas Rushdoony, "The Cult of Victimization," Position Paper No. 71, *Chalcedon,* P.0. Box 158, Vallecito, CA 95251.

16 Rousas Rushdoony, "Loyalties," Position Paper No. 62, *Chalcedon.*

17 Charles Sykes. A Nation of Victims. New York: St. Martin's Press, 1992, p. 18.

18 *Ibid.*

19 Torrey, *op. cit.*, pp. 175-176.

20 *Ibid.*, p. 176.

21 Ibid., p. 161.

22 *Ibid.*, p. 177.

23 Robitscher. *op. cit.*, pp. 162-163.

24 Peter Breggin, "Misuse of Psychiatric Drugs-East and West," *Esalen Catalog,* September 1985-February 1986, p. 7.

25 Larry Thomas, "Alcoholism Is Not a Disease," *Christianity Today,* October 4, 1985, p. 15.

Chapter 8 Organically Generated Difficulties

1 Stuart Scott and Heath Lambert, eds. *Counseling the Hard Cases: True Stories Illustrating the Sufficiency of God's Resources in Scripture.* Nashville, TN: B&H Publishing Group, 2012, p. 301. Hereafter page references to this book will be in parentheses within the text.

2 Martin and Deidre Bobgan. *Counseling the Hard Cases: A Critical Review.* Santa Barbara, CA: EastGate Publishers, 2016, pp. 47-68.

3 Jay E. Adams. *Competent to Counsel.* Grand Rapids, MI: Baker Book House, 1970, pp. 28-29.

4 Heath Lambert, "Can Jesus Heal Mental Illness?" Part 3, Biblical Counseling Coalition, May 16, 2014, http://biblical counselingcoalition.org.

5 E. Fuller Torrey, email 9/13/2014.

6 Erno Daniel. *Stealth Germs in Your Body.* New York: Union Square Press, 2008, p. 195.

7 *Ibid.,* pp. 196-197.

8 Erich Kasten, "Ruled by the Body," *Scientific American Mind,* Vol. 22, No. 1, p. 53, 54.

9 Melinda Beck, "Confusing Medical Ailments With Mental Illness," *Wall Street Journal,* August 9, 2011, p. D-1.

10 "Idiopathic," www.en.widipedia.org/wiki/Idiopathic.

11 Robert M. Johnson. *A Logic Book,* 2nd Ed.. Belmont, CA: Wadsworth Publishing Company, 1992, p. 248.

12 *Blues Buster,* Vol. 2, No. 11, p. 1.

13 Harvard Mental Health Letter, Vol. 19, No. 7, p. 1.

14 K. Pajer et al., "Discovery of blood transcriptomic markers for depression in animal models and pilot validation in subjects with early-onset major depression," *Translational Psychiatry,* 4/17/2012, http://www.ncbi.nlm.nih.gov/pubmed/22832901; Marla Paul, "First Blood Test to Diagnose Depression in Adults," www.northwestern.edu; "New Blood Test Can Identify Depression, *Mind, Mood & Memory,* December 2014, p. 2.

15 Bobgan, *Counseling the Hard Cases: A Critical Review, op. cit.,* p. 193.

Chapter 9 Sin-Saturated Counseling

1 Lawrence Le Shan, *Association for Humanistic Psychology,* 1984, p. 4.

2 Martin and Deidre Bobgan. *Against "Biblical Counseling": For the Bible.* Santa Barbara, CA: EastGate Publishers, 1994.

3 Charles J. Sykes. *A Nation of Victims.* New York: St. Martin's Press, 1992, p. 11.

4 *Ibid.,* pp. 14-15.

5 *Ibid.,* p. 15.

6 David Powlison, "Cure of Souls (and the Modern Psychotherapies)," www.ccef.org/cure-souls-and-modern-psychotherapies.

7   Jay E. Adams. *Update on Christian Counseling*, Vol. 1 and 2. Grand Rapids: Zondervan, 1977, 1979, 1981, Introduction to Vol. 2.

8   Jay E. Adams. *Competent to Counsel*. Grand Rapids, MI: Baker Book House, 1970, p. xv.

9   Jay E. Adams. *The Case of the "Hopeless" Marriage: A Nouthetic Counseling Case from Beginning to End*. Stanley, NC: Timeless Texts, 2006. Subsequent references appear in the text with page numbers.

10 "Born Again Adults Less Likely to Co-Habit, Just as Likely to Divorce," Barna Research Online, August 6, 21001, www.barna.org.

11 Brent Atkinson, "Brain to Brain," *Psychotherapy Networker*, Vol. 26, No. 5, p. 40.

12 Martin and Deidre Bobgan. *Person to Person Ministry: Soul Care in the Body of Christ*. Santa Barbara, CA: EastGate Publishers, 2009, pp. 56-59.

13 *Ibid.*, p. 64.

14 Holly Sweet, "Women Treating Men," *Psychotherapy Networker*, Vol. 34, No. 3, p. 34.

15 David Wexler, "Shame-O-Phobia," *Psychotherapy Networker*, Vol. 34, No. 3, p. 23

16 Terrence Real quoted by Carl Sherman, "Man's Last Stand," *Psychology Today*, Vol. 37, No. 4, p. 71.

17 Gary R. Brooks. *A New Psychotherapy for Traditional Men*. San Francisco: Jossey-Bass Publishers,1998, pp. 41, 42.

Chapter 10 Christian Response to Mental Illness: Mutual Care in the Body of Christ

1   This section titled "Person to Person Ministry" is reprinted from from Martin & Deidre Bobgan. *Person to Person Ministry: Soul Care in the Body of Christ*. Santa Barbara, CA 93110: EastGate Publishers, 2009. pp. 229-232.

Made in the USA
Middletown, DE
03 September 2023

37882801R00129